# With Cloak and Dagger

## H. H. Meyers

# WITH CLOAK AND DAGGER

## CONTENTS

# PREFACE

This book is written for generic Seventh-day Adventists – those within the denomination of that name and equally, those who are numbered among the increasing groups of believers who, by conscience or expulsion, find themselves outside the pale of the denomination.

The author does not presume to engage in a definitive defence of historic Seventh-day Adventism - inspiration and libraries of Adventist publications do just that, adequately. This book will demonstrate that basic fundamental principles which were endorsed by God's prophet to His remnant church as having "unquestionable authority", have since been systematically eroded and even changed. It explains how this change has been made possible and is now being consolidated by a system of church administration which has been set in place contrary to the expressed will of God.

As the readers progress through these pages, they will notice how the church's failure to heed the warnings of its prophet, Mrs E.G. White, repeatedly prove her dictum that **"a backsliding church lessens the distance between itself and the Papacy"**.

The author, who is an Australian, has been an Adventist all his life. Therefore many of the illustrations used in support of his propositions are drawn from his own knowledge and experiences within the South Pacific Division.

Many of our readers will note a similarity of conduct in their own country, some even having experienced the heavy hand of state-assisted persecution.

Sadly, many precious souls are now being admitted into church membership with a limited knowledge of Adventism. Increasingly, many of these people are further disadvantaged as they train to take up positions in our ministry and educational system, that seem bent on exchanging the "testimony of Jesus" for the "doctrines of men". With such people in mind, the author has included an extensive appendix which will give them an insight into the true position of Adventism on Christ and His ministry.

It is the sincere desire of the author that this humble attempt to arouse God's people from their Laodicean dreamtime will reawaken in the reader that burning commitment which the pioneers so gladly exhibited in taking to a judgment-bound world the "everlasting gospel", as found in the revelation of Jesus. We can then pray with sincerity, "Even so, come, Lord Jesus. AMEN".

The Author

# CHAPTER 1

# THE EXPERTS

The late Donald G. Barnhouse read a copy of that Seventh-day Adventist classic, Steps to Christ. This is a book that has led innumerable people to accept the Lord Jesus Christ as their personal Saviour. Many servicemen during two world wars treasured its precious message which brought hope and comfort to their uncertain existence. It made quite an impression on Dr Barnhouse, so much so, that he gave the book prominent mention in his evangelical magazine Eternity, June 1950. Under the heading "How to Read Religious Books" he claimed that reading such a book with its "half-truths and Satanic error" was akin to a worm on a hook, "the first bite is all worm, the second bite is all hook, that is the way the Devil works". It is not surprising then, that he referred to its author Mrs E.G. White, as "the founder of a cult".

Apparently, such a vicious attack on a church which claimed to be christian provided no impediment to the growth of one of Protestantism's most popular magazines.*   Such pronouncements 1. evidently accorded with acceptable Christianity. For, were not Seventh-day Adventists just another cult? They were credited with believing that Jesus Christ was a sinner, and denying His completed work of salvation at the cross. They were legalists who believed in salvation by works, part of which was the keeping of the Biblical Sabbath day. And, to cap it off, they had the temerity to claim that they were God's remnant church on whom God had bestowed the gift of prophecy! Yet, within six years, Dr Barnhouse was able to declare: (Eternity, Sept. 15, 1956)

-1-

I should like to say that we are delighted to do justice to a much-maligned group of sincere believers, and in our minds and hearts take them out of a group of utter heretics to acknowledge them as redeemed brethren and members of the body of Christ.

Yes, he was referring to the Seventh-day Adventist Church! Our leaders were ecstatic. Adventists could now hold their heads high as Christendom extended their brotherly arms to welcome them into the fold.

What had brought about this dramatic change? Had Barnhouse seen the light or had Adventism changed its "unchristian" views? Let Dr Barnhouse provide some clues. On the 16th May 1958, while in conversation with Adventist layman Al Hudson, Barnhouse said:

I hate Saturday as a Sabbath religious day. I hate it because God hates it. (As Reported in Pilgrims Rest DH 115, p.1)

On Adventists' belief that they are the remnant church, Barnhouse said:

If you believe that, you are a megalomaniac.(Ibid)

He went on to comment on the prolific pen of Mrs White:

That's too much you know. She was running off at the mouth, and the Holy Spirit certainly was not doing it. (Ibid p.2)

And again:

God Almighty never spoke through a woman. (Pilgrims's Rest DH 114, p.1) You [SDAs] were founded on a lie. (Ibid p.2)

The Editor of Barnhouse's *Eternity* magazine

was Dr Walter Martin. While lecturing in the Christian Mission Church, Napa, California, as recently as 22 Feb.1983, on the subject of Seventh-day Adventist beliefs, he declared:

> There is no need for any investigative judgment at any time because Jesus took care of it all at the cross.

Obviously, the three angels of Revelation 14 had failed to impress Messrs Barnhouse and Martin. During the late fifties, as a result of some eighteen months of intense dialogue with high-ranking representatives of the Seventh-day Adventist church, Barnhouse had insisted that Adventists publish their doctrinal beliefs. This they did under the title, Seventh-day Adventists Answer Questions On Doctrine, [QOD].(Review & Herald Publishing Association,1957)

This book became our passport to Christendom and enabled Dr Barnhouse to boast that he and Martin had changed the theology of a whole denomination! (See Eternity, Sept 1956, pages 6,7, 43,45). Repeatedly we are told by Adventist leadership that we have not deviated from historical Adventism. In the Introduction to Questions On Doctrine, we read: "This was not to be a new statement of faith." The writers, counsellors and editors "have labored conscientiously to state accurately the beliefs of Seventh-day Adventists." (p.8)

But shortly after proclaiming Adventists as part of the Christian community, Barnhouse, in commenting on Questions On Doctrine, was led to observe:

> Let's face it, in a very nice way, the leaders who have written this book, have moved from the traditional position of the S.D.A. movement. They've come back toward the Bible.

-(<u>Pilgrims Rest</u> DH 114, p.3)

Here is a serious anomaly which questions the integrity of our leadership. Seventh-day Adventists have been welcomed into the fraternity of Christendom on the basis of change. Our leaders claim that we have not changed! Has Christendom been duped? Have members of the S.D.A. church become victims of the greatest confidence trick since Jacob awoke to find himself in bed with Leah?

*1. <u>Eternity</u> magazine ceased publication while this book was being written.
Shortly after, its one-time editor, Dr Walter Martin passed away.

# CHAPTER 2

# "750 PAGES FULL OF WONDERFUL TRUTH"

After Questions On Doctrine was published by the Review & Herald Publishing Association in late 1957, General Conference President, Reuben R. Figuhr was so proud of it that he claimed it to be the most significant achievement during his term of office.

Yet Dr B.G. Wilkinson, veteran minister of the SDA church, College administrator and author of the scholarly books, Truth Triumphant and Our Authorized Bible Vindicated had a decidedly different view. After reading the manuscript of QOD he is reported to have described it as a dagger aimed at the heart of the Seventh-day Adventist church.(Recorded interview, Mike Clute)*    1.

The General Conference subsidised the cost of this book in order to ensure it would be widely distributed amongst non-Adventists. However, when it was offered to Adventists in Ministry magazine as "750 pages full of wonderful truth," the price was $US5.00.

But surprisingly, no one wanted his name connected with QOD for we are told only that it was "Prepared by a representative group of Seventh-day Adventist leaders, Bible teachers and editors". We are also told that the book came into being to meet a definite need" (QOD p.7), that a large Protestant publisher in the United States wanted to publish a book in which would be presented a general view of our history and beliefs, that the publishers approached the General Conference for information which resulted in an extensive search of our denominational

literature and that there followed a series of
meetings drawn out for over a year with the un-
named members of the committee. (See Ibid)

What we are not told is that the publisher
was Dr Donald Barnhouse, a champion of popular
evangelical thought. Neither are we told that he
had absolutely no time for Seventh-day Adventism. He had commissioned fellow evangelical, Dr
Walter Martin, to expose our denomination as a
cult.   It was Martin who insisted that he research his subject thoroughly by requesting dialogue with General Conference officers and that
he have access to our literature.

Subsequent to the ensuing meetings and publication of QOD, some participants have revealed
the names of the GC Conferees. They were elders:

T.E. Unruh, President of East Pennsylvania Con-
               ference
L.E. Froom, General Conference Field Secretary
R.A. Anderson, Ministerial Secretary, Editor
               Ministry
W.E. Reed, General Conference Field Secretary
           (Reported by T.E. Unruh, published by
           Pilgrims Rest DH 101,102)

These gentlemen were so amiable to their
would-be inquisitors that the Evangelicals were
soon disarmed and within a very short time were
on their knees praying for Christian unity!

As a result of these meetings, Barnhouse and
Martin were assured that Seventh-day Adventists
were now sufficiently theologically tuned to
popular evangelicalism to be regarded as Christians. So a deal was struck. If Adventists would
publish satisfactory answers to some forty-eight
questions, Eternity magazine would not expose us
as a cult, but would instead,  declare us to be

part of the Christian community. Barnhouse and Martin even offered to help out where we had difficulty in translating our "quaint" theological terminology into understandable Christian language!

The book, Questions On Doctrine, was the result. We were declared to be truly Christian by people whom President Figuhr obviously admired as exponents of Christianity and as authorities on cultism. Was his confidence misplaced? We shall see.

When Walter Martin was later questioned about Roman Catholicism's standing in the cultist world, he replied: "Roman Catholicism is not a cult". Then he sought to preserve some credibility by adding, "But within the Roman Church there are cults, such as the cult of Mary. But the basic doctrines of the Roman Catholic Church are Christ's Catholic theology to which most Protestants subscribe." Do Evangelicals no longer subscribe to the basic Christian belief that there is "one mediator between God and men, the man Christ Jesus?" 1 Timothy 2:5

* 1. On January 14, 1985, Evangelist Mike Clute recorded an interview with a friend of the Wilkinson family. Says Clute:

"Of course, the gentleman whom I interviewed does not want his name disclosed or else he would have done so at the time of the interview."

(Letter to Author July 8, 1989)

To faithful Seventh-day Adventists back in the mid-fifties it was a fearful doctrinal crisis in our Church. But to the believers in our day it is now seen to have marked the beginning of the end.

For the errors that the so-called "Evangelical Conferences" brought into our denomination grew throughout the sixties and seventies and were used by modernists in our Church, such as Desmond Ford, to lay a solid foundation for what is now called the "new theology"...

At that time, certain Evangelical Protestants asked a small group of our leaders to reconsider the stated doctrinal beliefs of our denomination— and, if possible, to restate them in "theological terms" that would be acceptable to the Protestant world around us. This seemed but a small concession in view of the golden opportunity held out before us: unity and fellowship with the other Protestant Churches is not one of the objectives of the Second Angel's message of Revelation 14:8, much less that of the Third Angel which follows it...

— Vance Ferrell
"The Beginning of the End" DH 101.

# CHAPTER 3

# "CRISIS" HE CRIED!

The casual reader of Questions On Doctrine could be excused for not noticing any startling change in Adventist doctrine. Indeed, we are assured in the introduction that "this volume can be viewed as truly representative of the faith and beliefs of the Seventh-day Adventist Church. (pp 8,9)

But some who were in a position to know claim that the original manuscript contained a great deal of error. It had to be toned down before those concerned with its printing would accept it. As one observer put it:-

> The book editors at Review & Herald could not swallow it. And so it went back to the General Conference for further revisions. This is why the book is so mixed up... The heresy was then more carefully worded to slip by the Review book editors. (Pilgrim's Rest DH104)

This is probably why it became acceptable to Martin and Barnhouse and yet did not immediately raise too great a storm among Adventists, especially amongst the ministry, the majority of whom were working long hours while conscientiously carrying out their chosen task of spreading the everlasting gospel.

We have already mentioned Dr B.G. Wilkinson's reaction. Unfortunately we do not have a record of his thoughts in writing. But one retired veteran of the ministry, also a scholar, teacher and author, has recorded his opinion of Questions On Doctrine. He is Elder M.L. Andreasen, described in the SDA Encyclopedia as an authority on our sanctuary message.*     1.

Having read the manuscript of <u>QOD</u>, he repeatedly protested to General Conference President
Figuhr, concerning changes to our doctrines.
After being curtly rebuffed, he wrote and circulated several open letters which were subsequently gathered together and published under
the title of <u>Letters to the Churches</u>.* Andreasen
warned:     2.

> We have reached a crisis in this denomination
> when leaders are attempting to enforce false
> doctrine and threaten those who object.  The
> whole programme is unbelievable. Men are now
> attempting to remove the foundation of many
> generations, and think they can succeed.  If
> we did not have the Spirit of Prophecy, we
> would not know of the departure from sound
> doctrine which is now threatening us and the
> coming of the Omega which will decimate our
> ranks and cause grievous wounds. The present
> situation has been clearly outlined.  We are
> nearing the climax. (<u>Letters to the Churches</u>
> No 3)

As a reward for his pains, the Conference
rescinded Elder Andreasen's ministerial credentials and deprived him of his sustentation! When
the poor man applied to the government for re-
lief money, the Social Welfare men contacted our
administrators who were shamed into restoring
his allowance.

Elder Andreasen was an elderly man.  As this
champion of the faith lay broken-hearted on his
deathbed, rejected and punished by the leadership of his beloved church, we can only imagine
his anguish as he contemplated the fulfilment of
Mrs White's prophecy:

> Books  of a  new order  would be  written.  A

system of intellectual philosophy would be introduced... Nothing would be allowed to stand in the way of the new movement. (<u>Special Testimonies</u> Series B, No 2,pp.54, 55)

Or perhaps he would attempt to answer Mrs White's rhetorical question pertaining to the Alpha of apostasy and apply it to the beginning of the Omega:*

What influence is it that would lead men at this stage of our history to work in an underhanded, powerful way to tear down the foundations of our faith — the foundation that was laid down in the beginning of our work by prayerful study of the word and by revelation? (<u>Ibid</u>)

As we proceed, we shall seek to discover the answer to this question. We shall reveal the "underhanded" way in which a mere handful of men set themselves up as expositors of our faith and interpreters of the Spirit of Prophecy. We shall see how, under the protection of sympathetic presidents, they have literally "torn down the foundations of our faith."

*1. Andreasen gave special study to the doctrine of the sanctuary and was considered an authority in that field. (SDA Encyclopedia 1976 p. 43)

*2. <u>Letters to the Churches</u> under the title, <u>The Witness That Our Fathers Bore</u>, is available from Pr G. Burnside, 95 Brown's Rd, WAHROONGA, N.S.W.2076. Australia

*3. Referring to Sister White's remarks on books of a new order and the underhanded tearing down of the foundations of our faith, Andreasen said:
"All this was written to meet the apostasy in the Alpha period. We are now in the Omega period which Sister White said would come." (<u>Letters to the Churches</u> No 6)

Important truths concerning the atonement are taught by the typical service. A substitute was accepted in the sinner's stead; but the sin was not canceled by the blood of the victim. A means was thus provided by which it was transferred to the sanctuary. By the offering of blood, the sinner acknowledged the authority of the law, confessed his guilt in transgression, and expressed his desire for pardon through faith in a Redeemer to come; but he was not yet entirely released from the condemnation of the law. On the day of atonement the high priest, having taken an offering from the congregation, went into the most holy place with the blood of this offering, and sprinkled it upon the mercy-seat, directly over the law, to make satisfaction for its claims. Then, in his character of mediator, he took the sins upon himself and bore them from the sanctuary. Placing his hands upon the head of the scapegoat, he confessed over him all these sins, thus in figure transferring them from himself to the goat. The goat then bore them away, and they were regarded as forever separated from the people.

Such was the service performed "unto the example and shadow of heavenly things".

E.G. White
Great Controversy, p 420.

# Chapter 4

# THE DAGGER

---

Few Seventh-day Adventists in 1956 knew of the events which have since come to be known as the Evangelical meetings. They were cloaked in official secrecy. It was left to Dr Barnhouse to drop what he called a bombshell, in September of that year. He published an article in Eternity magazine titled, "Are Seventh-day Adventists Christians?" (At the following General Conference session in 1958, the meetings were officially ignored.)

Speaking of the second meeting with the G.C. Conferees, Barnhouse wrote:

> It was perceived that the Adventists were strenuously denying certain doctrinal positions which had previously been attributed to them. For instance, they stated that "they repudiated absolutely the thought that Seventh-day Sabbath keeping was a basis for salvation..." and later in his report, "that Sabbath keeping is in any way a means of Salvation." (Eternity, September 1956)

When Walter Martin pointed out to them that we had published teachings considered by Christendom to be anti-Christian, they professed surprise and, "immediately brought the fact to the attention of the General Conference officers that this situation might be remedied and such publications be corrected" (Eternity, Sept.1956 p.6)

Barnhouse then reveals that the "same procedure was repeated regarding the nature of Christ while in the flesh, which the majority of the

denomination has always held to be sinless,
holy, and perfect, despite the fact that certain
of their writers have occasionally gotten into
print with contrary views completely repugnant
to the church at large".* They further explained    1.
to Mr Martin that they had among their number,
members of the "lunatic fringe" even as there
are similar wild-eyed irresponsibles in every
field of fundamental Christianity. (Ibid p.7)

Of our Sanctuary belief, Barnhouse reported:
> They [the GC conferees] do not believe as
> some of their earlier teachers taught, that
> Jesus' atoning work was not completed on Cal-
> vary but instead, that He was still carrying
> on a second ministering work since 1844.*    2.
> This idea is absolutely repudiated. They
> believe that since His ascension, Christ has
> been ministering the benefits of the atone-
> ment which He completed on Calvary. (Ibid)

So this is how Christendom at large and some
SDA church members came to know of the historic
meetings.   Certainly, few Adventists realised
that the doctrinal pillars of our faith were
being traded for the smile of Christendom. Let
us just summarize the understanding given by our
leaders to Barnhouse and Martin and square it
off with sound Adventist teaching.

**1. That Sabbath keeping is not in any way a
means of salvation.**
It is quite true that Sabbath observance is
no guarantee of salvation.   But it is equally
true that those who have a knowledge of Sabbath
truth and ignore it, will not be saved:
> The keeping of the Sabbath is a sign of loy-
> alty to the true God... It follows that the
> message which commands men to worship God and

keep His commandments, will especially call upon them to keep the fourth commandment. (Great Controversy p. 438)

Sabbath observance is eternal:
And it shall come to pass, that from one new moon to another, and from one Sabbath to another, shall all flesh come to worship before Me, saith the Lord. (Isaiah 66:23)

So we see that the conferees failed to uphold the message of the first angel of Rev.14, and showed a reckless disregard for the dire warning of the third angel (Rev. 14:7,9,10)

**2. That the majority of SDAs had always held that the incarnate Christ had a nature which was "sinless, holy and perfect" while the views of a minority, the "lunatic fringe" were "repugnant".**

Here we come face to face with a statement which can only be resolved by arriving at one of two conclusions. Either these men had very short memories or they were deliberately deceiving the evangelicals. Either way, they disqualified themselves as competent representatives of the Seventh-day Adventist Church. Here are a few pertinent facts which will help readers to reach their own conclusions.

Just five years prior to the Evangelical meetings, Elder W.E. Read (one of the conferees) had quoted Sister White in a G.C. Bulletin, 1950 p. 154:

Jesus was in all things made like unto His brethren. He became flesh even as we are.

This was just one of a plethora of statements in Adventist literature upholding the Biblical concept of a Saviour who came to this earth through the seed of Abraham and "was in all points tempted like as we are, yet without sin." (Heb. 4:15)

Dr Ralph Larson, in his monumental thesis, The Word Was Made Flesh, details some four hundred written statements by Mrs E.G.White and approximately eight hundred statements by other SDA writers on Christ's earthly nature. Over a period of one hundred years of SDA writers, Dr Larson was able to find no statement that Christ received the sinless nature of unfallen Adam, as claimed by Barnhouse. Our leading doctrinal book Bible Readings for the Home Circle, published in the year of Mrs White's death (1915), had sold by the million. It stated:

> In His humanity Christ partook of our sinful human nature. If not, then He was not made "like unto His brethren", was not "in all points tempted like as we are", did not overcome as we have to overcome... Christ inherited just what every child of Adam inherits, — a sinful nature. (p. 174)

And on page 236 we read:

> By the dogma of the immaculate conception of the Virgin Mary...modern Babylon teaches that God, in the person of His son, did not take the same flesh with us;that is, sinful flesh.

Yet it is inconceivable that these conferees were not aware that in the 1949 edition of Bible Readings, the "sinful nature" of Christ had been quietly deleted. How then could these men honestly claim to represent historic Seventh-day Adventist beliefs? As for Read, he had to do a complete somersault by refuting his previous position, in order to get out of the "lunatic fringe" and be eligible to join that elite Washington club of "sane leadership".

**3. A new doctrinal position for Adventism or merely the position of a few who saw themselves as the "sane leadership" of Adventism?**

As we have seen, these conferees did not represent a majority group. They were a mere handful of men from the General Conference who were handpicked by a sympathetic G.C. president. As to whether or not they represented sane leadership, it is debatable. One thing we do know, they considered themselves sufficiently sane to judge Mrs E.G. White, along with the vast majority of past and contemporary Adventist writers as part of the "wild-eyed, lunatic fringe".

**4. They repudiated the belief of some of our earlier teachers that Jesus' atoning work was not completed at Calvary, but was still going on in heaven.**

It was not just "some of our earlier teachers" that believed in Christ's continuing atonement. It had been consistently taught since pioneer days and was backed solidly by our leaders and the Spirit of Prophecy.

Elder A.G. Daniells was General Conference President during the years 1901-1922, and under his leadership, Bible Readings for the Home Circle was offered extensively to the public as representative of Adventist belief. Of the atonement in type and antitype it stated:

> In the heavenly sanctuary the sacrifice is offered but once; and but one atonement or cleansing of the heavenly sanctuary can be made, which must take place at the time assigned by God for it. And when the great atonement, or cleansing of the heavenly sanctuary has been made, God's people will be forever free from sin and the fate of all will be forever sealed.(See Rev. 22:11) This,

as in the type, will be a day of judgment. (p. 243) [Note: This great truth has been deleted from the revised 1963 paperback edition of Bible Readings. So also has the key reference text of Dan. 8:14 and the year 1844 been deleted!]

While president of the General Conference, Elder C.H. Watson wrote a book, The Atoning Work of Christ, (R&H, 1934). The contents were accurately described by its title. He made it quite clear that Christ's work in heaven is a continuation of His atonement which was begun with His sacrifice:

> Most certainly by the great work of atonement, which by the sacrifice of Himself began at the cross, and was continued by His priestly ministry in the heavenly sanctuary until, in the judgment, sin's reign is ended. (p. 175).

To this could be added the supporting testimony of Elder M.L. Andreasen, and F.C. Gilbert's Messiah In His Sanctuary (R&H 1937). This concurs with the Spirit of Prophecy:

> Instead of the prophecy of Daniel 8:14 referring to the purifying of the earth, it was now plain that it pointed to the closing work of our High Priest in heaven, the finishing of the atonement, and the preparing of the people to abide the day of His coming. (Life Sketches of E.G.White p. 63)

So this is how the "experts" on Christianity and cults gave the world a grossly erroneous picture of the Seventh-day Adventist Church and its beliefs. Their aim was to show that we had changed our doctrines sufficiently to enable us to fit into their concept of Christianity.

Had the General Conference succeeded in fooling Barnhouse and Martin or had we indeed changed our beliefs?

*1. It is significant that Larson does not appear to find one written statement by Figuhr, Froom, Anderson or Unruh, expressing their views on the nature of Christ prior to the evangelical meetings. Apparently it was they who regarded our official view as repugnant, but, sensing their isolated position, they were not courageous enough to express their views publicly.

*2. It is interesting to note that, although the conferees did not fool their inquisitors, Questions On Doctrine was able to claim that it was not a "new statement of faith" (QOD p.8) without any apparent objection from Barnhouse and Martin.

"... The hitherto highly regarded 'Eternity' magazine devoted much of its space in its September, October, November 1956 and January 1957 issues to a defense of Seventh-day Adventism.

"...Let me state first, without equivocation, that I believe these editors who are thus interpreting present-day Seventh-day Adventism as 'evangelical' and advocating that the Christian church should receive its adherents with all of their heresies as 'brethren beloved', are utterly wrong, both in their methods and in their conclusions...

"Keep in mind that Seventh-day Adventism is not just a few 'big shots', but is composed of hundreds of churches and individual members. Even if these leaders were to repudiate some of their heresies, how about the local churches and their membership who have been 'brainwashed' for three generations with such teachings as that of annihilation of the wicked? Will they accept it from stem to circumference of the denomination because these leaders say it is not so any more?

"Now the question is: Will Mrs White have to go? Will the 'keystone of the arch' be removed and thus all the superstructure fall in a heap? This will have to be done if the heresies are abandoned, as 'Eternity' claims."

—Louis T Talbot,
"Why Seventh-day Adventism is Not Evangelical"
The King's Business, April 1957 pp. 23-30.

# Chapter 5

# THE CLOAK

---

Further articles on the Evangelical meetings continued to appear in succeeding issues of Eternity magazine. These were mostly concerned with justifying Eternity's conclusion that Adventists were now a truly Christian denomination, for the initial reaction among Protestantism was one of profound scepticism.

Christendom was also told that Adventists no longer regarded themselves as the remnant church but considered themselves only as part of the remnant church of God in the last days. And as for the gift of prophecy, Adventists did not regard the E.G. White Spirit of Prophecy counsels as in a class with the Bible prophets. They were regarded as counsels to Seventh-day Adventists only. (Eternity, Jan. 1957)

Such a generalised statement does not differentiate between special testimonies to the church and counsels as found in Steps to Christ, or books in the Conflict of the Ages series, all of which are eminently suitable for public outreach. When the General Conference published Questions on Doctrine, a book demanded by Christendom for Christendom in general, they did not hesitate to disregard their own statement by unselectively quoting Mrs White in order to get their points across! A quick glance through just the first twenty chapters shows that they not only quoted from books suitable for public use, but quoted from the following:-

Gospel Workers, Testimonies to Ministers, Early Writings, Counsels on Sabbath School Work, Counsels to Parents, Students and Teachers, Evangelism, Testimonies to the

Church Volumes 2,6,8 and even an E.G.W. Manuscript, No 18, 1899.

Such inconsistencies are common to those who wander into the shifting sands of conjecture, amendment and invention.

As news of the Evangelical meetings began filtering through the SDA church, it was deemed advisable to prepare the ministry for the forthcoming book, Questions On Doctrine. The church had a ready-made vehicle to carry out such a task--the Ministry magazine. All that was needed was a willing Editor and a supportive President. Both were in position - R.A. Anderson and R.R. Figuhr.*                                              1.

Editor Anderson had fielded an opening statement in the Ministry of December 1956, under the Editorial title, "Changing Attitudes Towards Adventism". He told of some recent articles concerning Adventists in leading religious journals and commented:

> When certain Christian leaders discovered recently that we believe absolutely in the sovereign deity of our Lord, in His pre-existence with the Father, in the absolute sinlessness of His nature during His incarnation on earth, in His all-sufficient atoning sacrifice on the cross, and in salvation by grace and by grace alone, then the basis of the misunderstandings which for a century have been a barrier between other Christian bodies and Adventists was removed. (p.17)

Evidently, "caution" was the watchword. Adventists should not be startled. Many of our ministers would need a careful conditioning process to have them readily accept Questions On Doctrine. Unlike the largely non-Adventist readership of Eternity, most Adventists were well

acquainted with our doctrines and had ready
access to our literature including the Spirit of
Prophecy.   So, in the foregoing quotation the
heresy of Christ's sinless nature was carefully
hedged about by our long-discarded vestiges of
Arianism, and the concept of a completed atonement was wrapped in an "all-sufficient atoning
sacrifice".

But it was left to L.E. Froom to undertake
the delicate task of turning our doctrines
around.*   His article "The Priestly Application    2.
of the Atonement Act" (February 1957) must, in
retrospect, be seen as about the greatest
exercise in manipulative semantics ever
attempted in Adventist literature.*   The opening   3.
statements were good solid Adventism. The closing statements contradicted them! (One wonders
if Barnhouse's "first bite all worm, second bite
all hook" remarks should not be re-directed to
this article!)

Here are Froom's opening remarks in which he
defines the term "atonement" correctly:

Despite the belief of multitudes in the
churches about us, it is not, on the one
hand, limited just to the sacrificial death
of Christ on the cross. On the other hand,
neither is it confined to the ministry of our
heavenly High Priest in the sanctuary above,
on the antitypical day of atonement – or hour
of God's judgment – as some of our forefathers first erroneously thought and wrote.

Instead, as attested by the Spirit of Prophecy, it clearly embraces both – one aspect
being incomplete without the other, and each
being the indispensable complement of the
other.(Ministry Feb. 1957 p.9)

Having thus made Adventists feel at ease with

his confirmation of a continuing work of atonement, Froom then gives a twist to what appeared
to be a perfectly plain statement. He does this
by mixing a contradiction with two truths:

> That is the tremendous scope of the sacri-
> ficial act of the cross — a complete, perfect
> and final atonement for man's sins. (Ibid.
> p.10)

Yes, it is true that the sacrifice was
complete and perfect. It is not true that the
atonement was final and complete and Froom had
correctly stated earlier that the atonement was
not "limited just to the sacrificial death of
Christ on the cross".

But wait, he has an explanation: "The atonement is two-fold; first a single comprehensive
act, then a continuing process or work of application." Thus our minds are conditioned to the
proposition that Christ is now administering the
benefits of an atonement completed at Calvary!
Christ's work of atonement which Mrs White said
began at the cross really means "completed"
according to Froom. That is the "hook".

How then could Froom possibly hope to fool
all those Adventists out there who knew very
well that the Spirit of Prophecy taught that the
investigative judgment, which is the cleansing
of the heavenly sanctuary, constituted the final
act of Christ's atonement?

He simply postulated an erroneous statement
as if it were fact:

> No doctrinal proof or prophetic interpreta-
> tion ever came to this people initially
> through the Spirit of Prophecy — not in a
> single case... The discovery and interpre-
> tation of Bible truth was always left for
> diligent Bible students. (Ibid. p.11)

Here is an emphatic enunciation of an entirely new principle for Seventh-day Adventists. Mrs
White never contributed any original doctrinal
material to our church!*  She was not a diligent  4.
student!  Apparently L.E. Froom saw himself as a
diligent student and therefore he was qualified
to interpret the Spirit of Prophecy; as witness,
this amazing dogmatic statement:

> Let there be no confusion then, over the term
> "making atonement" used by Ellen G. White in
> connection with Christ's priestly ministry in
> heaven - obviously meaning applying the com-
> pleted atonement to the individual. (Ibid p.
> 12)

Thus Froom effectively denies the principle
of the blood atonement which Christ is now applying in heaven on behalf of repentant sinners.
The blood emphasis is sadly lacking in this and
others of his writings on the heavenly
sanctuary, a fact which parallels popular Evangelicalism because of its belief that Christ
completed His work of salvation on Calvary.

*1 R.R. Figuhr had been associate editor of the Ministry
   magazine with R.A. Anderson who was G.C. Ministerial
   Secretary from 1950-1966.  Assuming that these men were
   attuned to each other's doctrinal wavelength, they now
   had the perfect set-up to superimpose mutual designs upon
   Adventism.
*2.Froom had been Ministerial Secretary from 1941-1950.
   During that time, Anderson had been his associate Editor
   of Ministry magazine.
   In his outstanding work "Beginning of the End", Vance
   Ferrell quotes a contemporary G.C. official who claimed
   that Anderson had told him personally that Froom "wanted
   to stand for the land-marks, but we told him that for
   the sake of fellowship with the Protestants, we must do

this.  This will bring in a new day for Adventists.  He (Froom) backed down so we could agree with the Evangelicals."  (<u>Pilgrims' Rest</u> DH 104)  But in the light of further material to be presented, it seems probable that Froom's reticence was due mainly to the fact that he might bear the blame for changing our doctrines.

*3.In the Dec. 1956 issue of <u>Ministry</u>, Froom had written an article, "The Atonement, The Heart Of Our Message", in which he stressed the importance of the atoning sacrifice and referred to Christ's High Priestly work as "ministering its provisions, benefits and effects to the beneficiaries of His grace — the subjects of His intercession".  (p.13)

*4.Many of our people do not realize how firmly the foundation of our faith has been laid.  My husband, Elder Joseph Bates, Father Pierce, Elder Edson, and others who were keen, noble and true, were among those who, after the passing of the time in 1844, searched for the truth as for hidden treasure.  I met with them and we studied and prayed earnestly... When they came to the point in their study where they said "We can do nothing more", the Spirit of the Lord would come upon me.  I would be taken off in vision and a clear explanation of the passages we had been studying would be given me...and I gave others the instruction that had been given me. (<u>Special Testimonies</u>, Series B, No 2, pp. 54, 57.)

# CHAPTER 6

# THE LAST DECEPTION

---

It is becoming quite evident that the G.C. conferees had certain problems in meeting the criteria demanded by apostate Protestantism. In short - how to deny the truth! It was one thing to tell the evangelicals to take no notice of the "wild-eyed lunatic fringe" of Adventism. It was an entirely different matter to tell that to Adventists. They couldn't! Not only would such "lunatics" have to include the majority of our past and then present leaders, but it must necessarily include God's prophet, Mrs E.G. White.

One solution to the Spirit of Prophecy hurdle was to destroy the effect of Mrs White's writings. Such a thought would be hardly original because she had warned already that this would happen:

> The very last deception of Satan will be to make of none effect the testimony of the Spirit of God. (Vol 1 Selected Messages p.48)

Nevertheless, as a result of the embarrassment over Spirit of Prophecy statements which conflicted with the views now being declared to the evangelicals, it was decided that two men should approach the E.G.White estate, search the Spirit of Prophecy writings for such statements and then attempt to neutralize them. An attempt to tamper with Mrs White's writings actually took place early in 1957, about the time that Eternity magazine was spreading the news of Adventism's "conversion" to Christianity. Providentially, someone saw fit to "leak" a copy of

the White Board of Trustees minutes for May 1957
and the recipient of those minutes was none
other than Elder Andreasen. (See Letters to the
Churches No. 2.)

As mentioned previously, Andreasen was considered by our denomination to be one of its foremost scholars on the sanctuary doctrine. He was
absolutely committed to the propagation and
maintenance of historic Adventism. Imagine his
chagrin when he read in these minutes that two
men had "suggested to the trustees that some
foot notes or appendix notes might appear in
certain of the E.G. White books clarifying very
largely in the words of Ellen G. White our
understanding of the various phases of the
atoning work of Christ" * (Minutes, p. 1483 as    1.
quoted by Andreasen in Letters to the Churches,
No.2)

What a suggestion! What an affront to Christ
and His messenger! And what a sad commentary on
the integrity of our leadership, that some
should confidently expect that such a dishonest
request could be even entertained, let alone
succeed! Not only were these men prepared to act
as interpreter to God's messenger, but they were
prepared to imitate her style of writing by
employing "the words of Ellen G. White" in order
that the deception might more readily succeed.*   2.

Andreasen was not the type of man to remain
silent, but he decided to follow Christ's
instruction to "speak to him alone". He wrote to
the chief officer, President Figuhr and this is
portion of the reply:

I am certain we can trust the brethren of the
White Estate to move cautiously in this
direction and not to take positions that
might be embarrassing in the future.
Certainly Brother Andreasen, there is no

intention here whatever to tamper with the writings of Sister White. We value them most highly. (<u>Letters to the Churches</u>, No.4)
(The reader will note the prime concern of the "Chief Officer" - it was not about the preservation of truth, but rather of any embarrassment which must inevitably follow a fraudulent action!)

Andreasen replied, pleading with Figuhr to "spare thy people, and give not thine heritage to reproach". He closed his letter with an expression of confidence in the President as he faced "the greatest apostasy the church has ever faced". (Ibid)

The President's reply, September 18, 1957:
I have considered the matter to which you referred closed. I do not believe that you have the right to use the Board Minutes of the White Estate as you have done. The Minutes are confidential and not intended for public use. I hope the time will never come when we take the position that men are to be condemned and disciplined because they come before properly constituted church Boards to discuss questions that they may have pertaining to the work and belief of the church". * (Ibid)

3.

In his reply, Andreasen noted that the president had condoned the two men's actions. He pointed out that he had used the information about the Minutes to inform him (Figuhr) alone, and that:
I consider the present instance the greatest apostasy that has ever occurred in this de-nomination, and this you would have kept

under cover!   And you have closed the door..
You are about to ruin the denomination.   I am
praying for you." (Ibid)

But Andreasen's pleadings with the president
were fruitless.   Figuhr was determined to stand
by his commitment to the Evangelicals. Here is
part of his response:

> This [Andreasen's activities] will place you
> in plain opposition to your church.  In view
> of all this, the officers, as I have previ-
> ously written, earnestly ask you to cease
> your activities" (Letters to the Churches,
> No. 4)

Andreasen did not cease his activities but
made his concerns public in what became known as
Letters to the Churches.   And so, as previously
noted, he was stripped of his credentials and
deprived of his sustentation.

Thus it can be seen that our leaders had made
no idle commitment to the Evangelicals as
reported in Eternity magazine when Barnhouse
said that they, meaning Adventist leaders, were:

> determined to put the brakes on any members
> who seek to hold views divergent from that of
> the responsible leadership of the denomin-
> ation. (Eternity EXTRA Sept. 1956 p.7)

No doubt, the spectacle of one of our most
respected veterans being persecuted for nobly
standing up and doing his God-ordained duty did
not pass unnoticed by other workers in the
church.  For most of them, it probably provided
a salutary lesson in obedience to man - a fact
which may explain the conduct of many to this
day.

*1. Andreasen claims that it was the editor of Ministry "who in his research became acutely aware of the E.G. White statements... and so he suggested that footnotes or appendix notes appear in certain of the E.G. White books.." (<u>Letters to the Churches</u>, No. 2) Later, in letter No. 5, Andreasen reveals that it was R.A.Anderson and W.E. Read who visited the White vault and proposed the insertions to her writings. W.E. Read had a long connection with the "Washington club", having experience as field secretary and chairman of the so-called Defence Committee.

*2. There are those who will mis-interpret the messages that God has given, in accordance with their spiritual blindness. (1 <u>Selected Messages</u> p.41)

*3. In spite of Figuhr's admission of these Minutes, the White Estate Board subsequently denied their substance in a circular letter dated 6 Sep. 1960 to all Divisions. (Reported by Pilgrims' Rest DH 103 p.3)

I was thoroughly shaken when I read the account of men attempting to have explanations and footnotes inserted into the White books to make it appear that she is in favor of, or at least not opposed to, the new doctrine that the aonement was made on the cross. I had been taught from my early connection with the church that those writings were of God, and must be revered highly. The idea that men might add or subtract, or in any way "explain" the writer's intent by adding "footnotes or explanations" never occurred to anyone.

After I had read the record of what took place, I did a deal of praying and meditation. What was my responsibility in this matter, or did I have any? I confided to no one. I decided my first responsibility would be to the officials in Washington. And so I wrote to headquarters. I was informed that I had no right to the information I had, for that was supposed to be secret, and I had no right even to read the documents.

After four letters were passed, I was informed that they did not care to discuss the matter further. The matter was settled. When I inquired if this meant that the door was closed, I received the reply: "I have considered the matter to which you have referred as closed."

> — Portions of Elder M L Andreasen's letter
> to Officers of General Conference,
> December 29, 1957.

# CHAPTER 7

# MOVEMENT OF DESTINY?

---

Even as Questions On Doctrine, with its dramatic breakthrough in public relations, was being presented throughout the world as a saviour of Adventism, opposition was steadily mounting. Andreasen's Letters to the Churches were having a telling effect in North America.*  1.

Walter Martin soon began receiving complaints from indignant Seventh-day Adventists. Not only did they repudiate the new doctrinal positions in QOD, but they claimed that Barnhouse and Martin had been hoodwinked by the General Conference men.

> This is not what the Adventist church really believes. You have been deceived...There are some important representatives of Seventh-day Adventism who are at this point beginning to move the denomination back from where they came in 1957. (Martin, Lecture Feb. 22, 1983, Napa, California)

In 1965, Walter Martin published his book, The Kingdom of the Cults. Pressure from sections of Protestantism to have Adventists re-declared a cult were again mounting. It had been noted that Adventists had discontinued publication of QOD and they had refused to sell Martin's book, The Truth About Adventism, in the Adventist Book Centres. Martin endeavoured to quieten the clamour by devoting a section of his book to Adventists. He admitted that conflicting views on Adventist belief were coming out in print, but stuck to his original contention that QOD was indeed a passport to Christianity. He quoted from the Review & Herald's claim:

> This book truthfully presents the theology
> and doctrine which the leaders of Seventh-day
> Adventism affirm they have always held.
> (Kingdom of the Cults p.369) *                        2.

The credibility of QOD was under severe scru-
tiny, both from within and outside our church.
Elder Froom, once so reticent [seemingly] to
undertake the task of altering our doctrines,
who with others had declined to have his name
appended to QOD, was by now sufficiently motiv-
ated and committed to openly defend the book and
expand considerably on its veiled heresies. His
book, Movement of Destiny, published in 1971 by
the Review & Herald Publishing Association did
just that.

It is probably fair to say that no other
Adventist publication has come with higher
credentials than this book. The Foreword bore
the imprimatur of G.C. President, R.H. Pierson*    3.
and the Preface appeared over the name of the
vice-president, Neal C. Wilson, the latter
having acted as chairman of the Guiding
Committee for Movement of Destiny. (The
Fascinating Story of MOD p.11) Said Wilson:

> We can see God's timetable and wisdom. He
> knew exactly when the Remnant Church, and its
> leadership would be under attack.* He knew    4.
> when the book would be needed most!. It will
> confirm our faith, it will rekindle the fires
> of dedication and commitment.." (MOD Preface)

With such illustrious credentials, Movement
of Destiny should be able to be read with the
utmost confidence by Seventh-day Adventists. Can
it?

In his opening remarks to the reader, Froom

deems it advisable to establish his authority for writing the book and to show that he was destined to bring to the Movement an under-standing of the Gospel which would lead it in-exorably on to victory. He reveals that his mandate came from none other than the late Arthur G. Daniells, president of the General Conference for some twenty-one years, and close associate of Mrs E.G. White. Said Froom:

> Back in the spring of 1930 ...[Daniells] told me he believed that at a later time, I should undertake a thorough survey of the entire plan of redemption – its principles, provi-sions and divine personalities – as they un-folded to our view as a Movement from 1844 onward, with special emphasis upon the deve-lopments of 1888 and its sequel. (MOD, p.17)

At the time of the 1888 General Conference session in Minneapolis, Daniells was serving in the mission field of New Zealand. But it seems that many years later, after being released from his long term as president of the General Conference, he had time to reflect on the main theme of the Minneapolis Conference – Righteous-ness By Faith. As a result, in 1926, he wrote the book Christ Our Righteousness. Froom claims that it was this work which Daniells wanted him to "round out in historical sequence what he had begun in 1926". (Ibid p.17) Froom continues:

> Daniells admonished me to be fair and faith-ful to fact, comprehensive and impartial in treatment, and to present the full picture in balance. 'Truth has nothing to fear', he admonished, 'and everything to gain'. (Ibid p.18)

Froom unequivocally accepts this challenge:

I must not be unfaithful to God and to the
Church, and the burden that has been placed
upon me.   That is how this portrayal came to
be written. (Ibid p.23)

As we examine some aspects of Movement Of
Destiny and look behind the scenes we shall keep
in mind Froom's commitment to truthfulness and
Daniell's maxam that "truth has nothing to
fear".We shall also seek to discover what President Wilson meant when he perceived the church
and its leadership to be under attack and perhaps even find out who its supposed enemies are.

*1. In Australasia, the membership, with its childlike trust
    in   General   Conference   leadership,   was   generally
    acquiesant. If and when Andreasen's activities were
    mentioned, it was usually in a derogatory manner.
*2. How could Martin keep foisting this untruth upon his
    readers when Barnhouse had claimed that they had changed
    the doctrines of a whole denomination? Note the discre-
    pancy:- "Let's face it ... the leaders who have written
    this book (QOD) have moved from the traditional position
    of the SDA movement." (Barnhouse)  This is confirmed by
    Anderson in a letter to Pastor Robert Greive, then
    President of the Queensland Conference.  After reading
    the manuscript for QOD, Greive wrote Anderson to see
    what was going on. Anderson replied, "Yes, we are trying
    to change the doctrines, but we want to take it to the
    Ministry before we go to the people with it." (Pilgrims'
    Rest DH 104)  And again, "While it is truth, we should
    be very careful not to set it before the laity until we
    are prepared to speak with a united voice." (Letter to
    Robert Greive, April 23, 1956)
*3. Although Pierson had strongly recommended MOD to all
    Seventh-day Adventists, he later had reason to change
    his mind.  In a letter dated Oct. 6, 1988 to the author
    (H. H. Meyers) he wrote, "Some portions of Elder Froom's

manuscript <u>Movement of Destiny</u> I had not read before its
publication... After reading some portions later, I
declined to have my Foreword included in any subsequent
editions." It is interesting to note that in a
subsequent edition of <u>MOD</u>, a new Foreword is written by
H.M.S. Richards. The Preface by Neal C. Wilson remains
intact.

*4. Elder Wilson does not identify the "attackers".

What greater deception could be foisted upon our people than for Satan to bring falsehood from within the church, while the members expect it to come from a source outside the church. How well we have been prepared to receive it by being taught to depend upon a system of religious organization to warn us of its approach and arrival, rather than encouraged to look to the platform of truth established in the early years of the movement. Even now, in this time of great peril, the leadership are foremost in cautioning against any discussion of the issues that are polarizing the membership. (See Review, May 24, 1979). They put forth the claim that there is a great deal more made of such situations than is called for; and if they, the leadership, are given the time to decide the conclusion of such issues, then all agitation will die down. Their admonition of caution, and many times silence, on life and death issues is a cry of peace and safety. Matters designed to stir the membership into action are, as a result, not heeded; and it is left to the leadership—the "dumb dogs" who never again lift up their voice like a trumpet to show God's people their transgressions..." (See 5T, p.211)—to decide for the membership what is and what is not the truth.

Jon A. Vannoy
"Under Which Banner?" 1981, p.81.

## CHAPTER 8

# "IMPEACHING THE DEAD"

---

Dr Le Roy Froom was very conscious of accusations against leadership. He had come in for his
fair share of censure for his part in what had
come to be seen by many as the evangelical sell-
out of the Fifties. Under the heading, "Unjusti-
fiable Charge of Leadership Unfaithfulness", he
says:

> Ever since the 1888 tensions there have been
> recurrent harpers on the note that the
> church, and primarily its leaders, actually
> rejected the message of 1888. (MOD p. 357)

If such charges had been recurring since
1888, how then would President Wilson see Movement Of Destiny as arriving just on time to meet
"God's timetable?" There must have been some
pressing and contemporary reason to which Wilson
was referring. Perhaps Froom can help us
further? He talks of the 1888 rejection charge
still persisting and refers to a recent call for
"retroactive" repentance in order that the Loud
Cry and Latter Rain should re-visit our Church.
Said Froom:

> Such a contention is a grave charge to be
> bandied about. If the charge is true, then
> there should be some clear-cut historical
> evidence. If not true, it "actually consti-
> tutes an impeachment of the dead", and "an
> explicit confession is due the Church today
> by promulgators of a misleading charge".(Ibid
> p.358)

Well, that surely does sound like enemies of
the Church at work, doesn't it? But worse still,

it sounds like the "enemies" are within our church!

It did not take long for the "mystery" to be made public. In November of 1972, there appeared a booklet titled, An Explicit Confession ...Due The Church, and it was signed by Donald K. Short and Robert J. Wieland, two Seventh-day Adventist ministers with extensive service in Africa and in their homeland, North America. Let us read from their introductory remarks:

> This public "confession" is made in response to a duty solemnly enjoined upon the authors of a private document. After twenty-two years of silence, they are now required to speak publicly, though they would prefer to remain silent.

> Their duty to "confess" is made clear by demands upon them published in Movement of Destiny and endorsed by the General Conference of Seventh-day Adventists. It is a duty the authors dare not evade. The Church will expect a sincere response to such an authoritative public charge. Truth requires it.

> Twenty-two years ago in the autumn of 1950, the authors prepared for the attention of the General Conference committee, a private manuscript entitled 1888 Re-Examined. Without the authors' consent or approval, this document with some six hundred Ellen G. White exhibits, was by others placed in the hands of an ever-widening circle of Seventh-day Adventist readers around the world. This is what has now been responsible for this public call to make An Explicit Confession.. Due The Church.

And what was 1888 Re-Examined all about? Again we quote from Short & Wieland:

> We said in 1950 that there is a neglected but

essential preparation to make before the
final outpouring of the Holy Spirit in the
Latter Rain can possibly come to enable the
Church to finish God's work on earth. That
most necessary preparation is recognition of,
and repentance for, the misunderstanding and
rejecting the "beginning" of the Latter Rain
and the Loud Cry. This "beginning", according
to Ellen G. White, was a message brought by
two young ministers to the 1888 General
Conference Session. Nearly one hundred times
in her writings she endorses this message and
the messengers in language never used at any
time about any other message or messengers.
For us now as a people to beg Heaven to give
us the Latter Rain, without recognizing this
obvious fact, is just as unreasonable as for
the Jews to keep on begging the Lord to send
them the Messiah without recognizing how He
kept His promise and did send Him two thous-
and years ago. (Ibid.)

In the rest of chapter 10 (MOD), Froom sets
out to show that the principles of the "1888
message" had indeed been adopted and put into
practice over the intervening years. He sees the
church's progress as evidence of the outpouring
of the latter rain. As further evidence he em-
barks on a recital of leaders' names who upheld
the principles of righteousness by faith including the "ultimate in leadership", Ellen G.
White.
Froom is in trouble! He is citing our
prophet's active role in promulgating righteousness by faith as proof that it had been
generally accepted by our leadership because she
herself was the "ultimate leader"!
But the argument does not fit the facts. Sis-

ter White had joined with Elders Waggoner and
Jones in travelling around the country with the
purpose of urging its acceptance! In 1890, she
was constrained to voice her concern in the
Review & Herald, 11th March, 1890:

> For nearly two years we have been urging the
> people to come up and accept the light and
> the truth concerning the righteousness of
> Christ, and they do not know whether to come
> and take hold of this precious truth.

Why were our people hesitant to accept the
message? She says:

> Our young men look to our older brethren and
> as they see that they do not accept the
> message, but treat it as though it were of no
> consequence, it influences those who are
> ignorant of the scriptures to reject the
> light. These men (the leaders) who refuse to
> receive the truth interpose themselves be-
> tween the people and the light. (R & H 18th
> March, 1890.

And why did our "older brethren" not accept
the 1888 message? In 1895, Mrs White wrote:

> Men who are entrusted with weighty responsi-
> bilities, but who have no living connection
> with God have been and are doing despite to
> His Holy Spirit... if God spares their lives,
> and they nourish the same spirit that marked
> their course of action both before and after
> the Minneapolis meeting, they will fill up to
> the full the deeds of those whom Christ
> condemned when He was upon earth. (Testi-
> monies To Ministers pp. 78,79)

So, with this mis-application of Mrs White's
concern - that the message of righteousness by

faith should take hold of our people – may we not well ask, **"Who is impeaching the dead?" and "Who is it that dares to impeach a prophet of God?"**

In 1926, over a decade after Mrs White's decease, were things any better? According to Elder Daniells they were not! In his book <u>Christ Our Righteousness</u>, we read:

> Through the intervening years (since 1888) there has been steadily developing the desire and hope – yes, the belief – that someday the message of righteousness by faith would shine forth in all its inherent glory, worth and power and receive full recognition.(pp.42,43)

After twenty-one years as General Conference president, Daniells was well qualified to speak on this subject. He was keenly aware of the opposition of which Mrs White spoke. Said he:

> The message has never been received, nor proclaimed, nor given free course as it should have been in order to convey to the church the marvellous blessings that were wrapped in it.(Ibid. p.47)

Those "marvellous blessings" would have automatically followed in the train of the latter rain had our leaders been receptive. Why then did Froom contradict his mentor, the very man whom he claims had commissioned him with the awesome responsibility of expanding on the work that he had commenced? Just listen to Froom:

> The denomination as a whole, and its leadership in particular, did not reject the message and provisions of righteousness by faith in and following 1888. (<u>MOD</u> p.370)

How then can Froom be claiming to be carrying

out Daniells' commission by contradicting him? Why does he attack two of God's faithful servants, Elders Short and Wieland, for sharing Sister White's and Elder Daniells' concerns? The answers to such questions do not come easily. It is not given to man to divine motives generated in the dark recesses of the heart. We can, however, examine the facts and learn from history.

Those who have read the books, Questions On Doctrine and Movement of Destiny must be struck with their similarities of format and literary style. Probably this is no mere coincidence, for Froom is given credit for writing most of QOD by none other than those whom the book was written to please – Barnhouse and Martin.* As one reads  1. through Movement of Destiny, it becomes increasingly clear that it is a defence of the evangelical meetings of the fifties and the doctrinal positions embraced in Questions On Doctrine.

At the time QOD was written, the price to the denomination appeared so high that no one was courageous enough to underwrite it. But after some fourteen years of exposure to its deadly heresies, Froom judged Adventists to have been sufficiently brainwashed for him to safely endorse the heresies in Movement Of Destiny with his own signature. But he did it under the guise of presenting true Adventism in the fullness of the 1888 message!

Conveniently, neither Mrs White nor Elders Waggoner and Jones were still around to object. Neither was Daniells, for that matter!

* 1.Veteran evangelist, Austin P. Cooke claims that while visiting in the USA in 1956, R.A.Anderson told him that he was involved in writing an important book concerning Adventist beliefs. Cooke believes this book was QOD. (Personal conversation with Author, 1988)

# Chapter 9

# THE 1888 MESSAGE (AND THE EVANGELICAL VIEW)

Let us briefly acquaint ourselves with the 1888 message of righteousness by faith which our prophet claimed is the "Third Angel's Message in Verity" (R&H April 1, 1890) and was the beginning of the latter rain. When Sister White heard Elder Waggoner's presentation at Minneapolis, she was estatic:

> ...it was the first clear teaching of the subject from any human lips I had heard, excepting the communication between myself and my husband. I have said to myself, it is because God has presented it to me in vision that I see it so clearly and they (its detractors) cannot see it because they have not had it presented to them as I have; and when another presented it, every fibre of my heart said Amen. (Manuscript 5, 1889)

Sister White, born Ellen Gould Harmon, was reared and baptized in Methodism. It would be fair to say that in the Christian world, Methodists had been champions of the Protestant dictum, **The just shall live by faith.** Unlike many of the reformationist churches, they stressed obedience to God's law as evidence of that faith.

Obviously then, Sister White was referring to a message that encompassed more than Wesley's understanding of the subject, for like Luther, Calvin and other reformers, he did not have an understanding of the three angels' messages as revealed to Seventh-day Adventists.

It was Elders E.J. Waggoner and A.T. Jones who picked up the threads of Protestantism's unfinished garment and interwove it with the fabric of the third angel's message. **It is this garment of Christ's righteousness which, if accepted by faith and worn in obedience, would enable the Seventh-day Adventist Church to give the message that would light the whole world with glory.** (The fourth angel of Rev. 18:1) This would be the inevitable result of the outpouring of the Holy Spirit, known as the latter rain. Said Mrs White:

> There are but few, even of those who claim to believe it, that comprehend the third angel's message; and yet this is the message for this time. It is present truth... Said my guide: There is much light yet to shine forth from the law of God and the gospel of righteousness. This message understood in its true character, and proclaimed in the Spirit will lighten the earth with its glory. (Ms.15, 1888;Olsen, p.296.Quoted in <u>1888 Re-Examined</u>)

That a true comprehension of the third angel's message would lead us to emphasize to the world the seriousness of living presently in the day of atonement, is made clear:

> We are in the day of the atonement, and we are to work in harmony with Christ's work of cleansing the sanctuary... We must now set before the people the work which by faith we see our great High-priest accomplishing in the heavenly sanctuary. (<u>R&H</u>, Jan. 21, 1890)

So it is abundantly clear that **the 1888 message of righteousness by faith is unique to Seventh-day Adventism. The message went much further than the Reformationist view which was** circumscribed "by faith alone". It was a message of faith that works, a faith that will enable us to obey and "follow Jesus in His great work of atonement in the heavenly sanctuary" (Great Controversy p.430)

It is obvious then, that those Seventh-day Adventists who deny Christ's continuing work of atonement, by claiming it was finished at the cross, are circumscribed by Reformationist theology. **Inevitably, they will increasingly hanker after the fellowship of those whose misunderstanding of the everlasting gospel they have followed.** How then can such leaders expect to be recipients of the latter rain and join with the fourth angel of Revelation 18 in the magnificent task of lighting the whole world with His glory?

False doctrine is one of the satanic influences that work in the church, and brings into it those who are unconverted in heart. Men do not obey the words of Jesus Christ, and thus seek for unity in faith, spirit, and doctrine. They do not labor for the unity of spirit for which Christ prayed, which would make the testimony of Christ's disciples effective in convincing the world that God had sent His Son into the world, "that whosoever believeth in Him should not perish, but have everlasting life." If the unity for which Christ prayed, existed among the people of God, they would bear living testimony, would send forth a bright light to shine amid the moral darkness of the world.

E.G. White
Testimonies to Ministers, p.48.

# CHAPTER 10

# THE DAGGER STRIKES (PART 1)

One of error's insidious traits is its penchant for free-loading on the back of truth. Its passage through Movement of Destiny is no exception. **If Adventism's doctrinal uniqueness is to be destroyed, then its very heart, the sanctuary message, must ultimately be targeted.** But the attack must not be too obvious.

Froom impressively announces the important truths of the sanctuary doctrine as being crucial to the very existence of Seventh-day Adventism:

> Any weakening or denial or submerging of the sanctuary truth is not only a serious, but a crucial matter. Any deviation or dereliction therefrom strikes at the heart of Adventism and challenges its very integrity. (Movement of Destiny p. 542)

Thus the reader's mind is lulled into a sense of false security. How many will not notice the gleam of a two-pronged dagger concealed beneath the cloak of truth?

The first prong is meant to destroy Adventism's belief in the true humanity of Christ during His incarnation - a humanity like ours in which He resisted sin and thus became our example; which in turn bestows on Him the Biblical qualification which befits Him to carry out the atoning work as our heavenly High Priest (See Hebrews 4:15)

An Editorial in the Review & Herald (Dec. 16, 1884) announcing a new edition of the book, The Atonement, by J.H. Waggoner, made this pertinent

observation linking Christ's human nature with
his qualifications as a High Priest:

> In (the atonement) is involved the great cen-
> tral "mystery" of the Gospel, "God manifest
> in the flesh", a divine being bearing the
> nature of the seed of Abraham...(As quoted in
> The Word Was Made Flesh p.42)

The second prong is meant to show that the
atonement was completed at Calvary in order to
satisfy the popular evangelical belief that
Christ's work of salvation was completed at the
cross. Therefore any future priestly ministry is
explained simply as the application of benefits
flowing from a completed atonement.

Let us examine the methods employed by Froom
in this two-pronged attack.

## 1. The "Vicarious" Humanity of Christ

Froom directs our minds to the time when a
few of our pioneers had brought some Arian views
to Adventism. Uriah Smith was one such person.

Elder E.J.Waggoner had dealt with this
diminishing problem at the 1888 Minneapolis
Conference by upholding Christ's deity as "all
the fulness of the Godhead", meaning of course
that Christ was an uncreated and eternal member
of the triune Godhead.

This position was always taken by Mrs White,
as coming out of Methodism, she had never held
Arian views.

But while the reader is left pondering over
the fact that some of our pioneers had been
wrong, Froom, by inference and timing, sets up
in the mind of the reader a link between
Christ's earthly nature and the fulness of the
Godhead. Referring to Waggoner's book, Christ
and His Righteousness, he says:

The full significance of Waggoner's highly significant descriptive concerning Christ's nature must not be missed. It is vital. He especially declared that Christ "is of the very substance and nature of God"!(<u>MOD</u> p.277)

Froom then quickly presses home his intent:

> Waggoner and his colleagues were moving definitely away from both the Arian and semi—Arian positions." (<u>MOD</u> p.278)

We are not aware that Waggoner had any Arian or semi—Arian views, but we do know that he believed that Christ took upon himself the nature of fallen humanity. Therefore it may appear to some that Froom is trying to show that those with similar views are hooked on a vestige of Arianism.

Then on page 318, in discussing the 1888 message of righteousness by faith, he says:

> It involved the very nature of Christ in whom the faith was to be invested.

Is Froom planting the idea in our minds that Waggoner, in rejecting Arianism, is repudiating the Biblical concept of a truly human Christ? We had better see just what Waggoner's position was:

> The spotless Lamb of God, who knew no sin was made to be sin. Sinless, yet not only counted as a sinner, but actually taking upon Himself sinful nature. He was made to be sin in order that we might be made righteousness.(<u>Christ and His Righteousness</u> pp 27,28)

But such a forceful declaration on Christ's humanity does not suit Froom. How does he over-come this problem? He simply resorts to a tactic with which he is becoming quite adept. He takes a few words and phrases from a statement and intersperses them with his own wording which when strung together, form a statement which obscures the intent of the original author.

Let's look at Froom's treatment of the last sentence of our quotation from Waggoner:

...He was actually "made" – vicariously – to "be sin for us" that we "might be made the righteousness of God in Him". (<u>MOD</u> p.197)

Notice Froom's insertion of the word 'vicariously'. This makes sheer mockery of the plan of salvation by attributing to Christ a make-believe human nature and constitutes blatant tampering with Waggoner's stated belief. Dr Larson, in his book <u>The Word Was Made Flesh</u>, cites from the 1891 G.C. Bulletin six instances in which Waggoner stated his position. They all accord with this sampling:

But what the law could not do, Christ came in the likeness of sinful flesh to do.
...Jesus was made in all things like unto those whom He came to save. (<u>The Word Was Made Flesh</u> pp 48,49)

During the two years following 1888, Mrs White gave unstinted support to Waggoner and Jones as they travelled about expounding on the theme of Christ's righteousness. In the <u>Signs of the Times</u>, 23rd Sept. 1889, she upheld Christ's true divinity and His acceptance of our fallen nature by saying:

He took upon Him our nature that He might reach man in his fallen condition.

And what about Jones? Did he share Froom's "vicarious" nature theory? Not at all! During his series of lectures on the third angel's message at the General Conference session of 1893, he made at least three statements similar to this:

> Ah, the Lord Jesus Christ, who came and stood where I stand, in the flesh in which I live, He lived there.(G.C. Bulletin 1893, p.412)

Let us remind our readers that Froom claims to be enlarging on the message commenced by Daniells in his book Christ Our Righteousness. With that goes the assumption that he is in agreement with Daniells' view of Christ's earthly nature. But this is not so. On page 38, Daniells quotes:

> Describe, if human language can, the humiliation of the Son of God, and think not that you have reached the climax, when you see Him exchanging the throne of light and glory which He had with the Father, for humanity. (Quoted from R&H Sep.11, 1888)

Is this Froom's "vicarious" or make-believe humanity that Daniells is describing? Certainly not! While ministerial secretary of the General Conference, Daniells had made his understanding plain:

> (He was made) like you, like me... Having triumphed over sin in sinful flesh ... (R&H Nov 7, 1929, p.5)

So it is clear that Froom is not fulfilling Daniells' commission (if indeed he had been commissioned), nor is he in agreement with the exponents of the 1888 message of righteousness by faith. (Whatever happened to Froom's commitment to truthfulness when he accepted Daniells' admonition "to be fair and faithful to fact"? See Chapter Seven)

Now we shall see how Froom tackles his biggest obstacle - the Spirit of Prophecy. Typically, he seeks the support of Mrs White, whom he lauds as "the peerless witness". (MOD chapters 28,29) Because her evidence happens to be in disagreement with Froom's "vicarious" or make-believe human nature of Christ, he resorts to what Dr Larson describes as "fraudulent" methods, and something which should be rectified by Adventists before our enemies expose this perfidy to world gaze. (See The Fraud of the Unfallen Nature, a pamphlet by Larson). Also, in his book, The Word Was Made Flesh, Dr Larson describes Froom's tactics as "a methodological monstrosity". (p.247)

One such tactic is to seek to interpret Mrs White's statements by supplying misleading sub-headings over her statements - a device which he apparently regarded as highly successful in the book Questions On Doctrine.

We shall mention here, just one example of several as exposed by Larson. On page 497 of MOD we find sub-heading No 5, **TOOK SINLESS NATURE OF ADAM BEFORE FALL.** There follows a veritable hotch-potch collection of words and phrases taken from nineteen Spirit of Prophecy quotations. No references are given. These are linked together by Froom's wording to make them appear to uphold the false declaration of his sub-heading.

In analysing these nineteen mini-quotes, Larson takes us to the source quotations and it soon becomes apparent that Mrs White said the opposite of what Froom is trying to make her say. Conveniently, Froom deletes the unwanted portions of her opening statement which provides the context. Here it is with the unwanted portion emphasized for identification:

> **In taking upon Himself man's nature in its
> fallen condition** [that is, after four thous-
> and years of sin], Christ did not in the
> least participate in its sin. (<u>1SM</u> p.256)

Needless to say, Froom astutely avoids such
forceful statements as:

> He humbled Himself, taking the nature of the
> fallen race... He knows by experience what
> are the weaknesses of humanity... and where
> lies the strength of our temptations...(<u>The
> Watchman</u> 3 Sept. 1907 p.563, as quoted in <u>The
> Word Was Made Flesh</u> p.146)

The second prong of the dagger will be
discussed in the following chapter.

We need to settle, every one of us, whether we are out of the church of Rome or not. There are a great many that have got the marks yet, but I am persuaded of this, that every soul who is here to-night desires to know the way of truth and righteousness (Congregation: Amen!), and that there is no one here who is unconsciously clinging to the dogmas of the papacy, who does not desire to be freed from them...

Suppose we start with the idea for a moment that Jesus was so separate from us, that is, so different from us that he did not have in his flesh anything to contend with. It was sinless flesh. Then, of course, you see how the Roman Catholic dogma of the immaculate conception necessarily follows. But why stop there? Mary being born sinless, then, of course, her mother also had sinless flesh. But you can not stop there. You must go back to her mother,...and so back until you come to Adam; and the result?—There never was a fall: Adam never sinned; and thus, you see, by that tracing of it, we find the essential identity of Roman Catholicism and Spiritualism...

E.J. Waggoner, as reported in General Conference Bulletin 1901, p.404.

# CHAPTER 11

# THE DAGGER STRIKES (PART 2)

---

## 2. "Atonement Completed at Calvary"

Having appeased the evangelicals, perhaps unwittingly, by robbing Christ of his qualifications to be our Heavenly High Priest (as in Heb. 2:17,18; Heb. 4:15), Froom now moves in to emasculate our sanctuary message by cutting the atonement off at the cross. But as long as Adventism continues to believe that the earthly sanctuary services were instituted to pre-figure the services of the sanctuary in heaven, this would be impossible.

So Froom sets about to distance the "earthly" from the "heavenly" by emphasizing that the earthly shadow was not an exact image. (See Heb. 10:1), (MOD p.558) Hopefully then, he can lead us to believe that the shadow was so distorted that all the atoning work of the earthly priesthood had no counterpart in heaven.

Ridiculous as this dis-similarity seems, this is exactly what Froom is about - not that he denies Christ's ministerial role in the heavenly sanctuary - he just insists that Christ is applying the benefits of a completed atonement. "The earthly was simply a figure for the time then present", he says. (MOD p. 557)

How differently the Lord's Messenger views type and anti-type!

> We are in the great day of atonement and the sacred work of Christ for the people of God that is going on at the present time in the heavenly sanctuary, should be our constant study. We should teach our children what the typical day of atonement signified, and that

it was a special session of great humiliation and confession of sins before God.  The anti-typical day of atonement is to be of the same character. (5T p.520)

How then, does our self-appointed exponent of righteousness by faith overcome the recurring obstacle of the Spirit of Prophecy?

He simply reverts to the old technique of interpreting the SOP to his own ends – a little more subjective selection and word manipulation arranged under misleading headings!  Let us take an example from page 501 of Movement Of Destiny. We have a sub-heading:-

COMPLETE ATONEMENT MADE ON CROSS under which we read:

When the Father beheld the sacrifice of His Son (on the cross) He said,'It is enough. The Atonement is complete'. And again, 'When He offered Himself on the cross, a perfect atonement was made for the sins of the people'.

And so on. From such fragments of SOP quotations Froom draws the conclusion:

The transaction of the cross then, is indis-putably the act of the atonement. (MOD p.501)

Once again, the references for these frag-mented quotations are withheld, and probably for very good reasons. How many of our readers would have the inclination or the facilities to source these quotations and check them out?  If we were to do so, it would become apparent that they were written in the context of the sacrificial aspect of the atonement. (The quotations come from R&H Sept.24, 1901 and the Signs of the Times June 28, 1899 respectively.)

When QOD had dealt with exactly the same quotations some fourteen years earlier, they had been correctly listed under the subheading: **COMPLETE SACRIFICIAL ATONEMENT MADE ON CROSS.** (QOD p.663)

If we are to believe that Froom was the main author and editor of QOD, it would seem that Froom's interpretative role had expanded considerably. What was then a "complete sacrificial atonement" had now become a "COMPLETE ATONEMENT"! (MOD p. 501)

Briefly, let us look at another of Froom's misleading sub-headings and garbled quotations:

**CROSS SOLE MEANS OF ATONEMENT.** The cross is thus the 'means of man's atonement'. There could have been 'no pardon for sin had this atonement not been made'. So, 'the cross was ordained as a means of atonement'. Christ 'gave Himself an atoning sacrifice'. (p.502)

It will be noticed that in spite of Froom's efforts, he does not succeed in making Mrs White state that the cross was the "sole means of atonement" (as in the sub-heading). She merely claims that it was "a means of man's atonement" - which of course, is quite correct. There can be no atonement in the heavenly sanctuary (as in the earthly) without the sacrifice which provides the blood. So once again, Froom devises an interpretative sub-heading as a substitute for fact.

No wonder he refrains from quoting Mrs White on the continuing atonement in heaven! In that marvellous work of inspiration, The Great Controversy Between Christ and Satan, she describes Christ's judicial mediatorial role which started at the close of Daniel's great time prophecy ending in 1844 (Daniel 8:14):-

Attended by heavenly angels, our great High Priest enters the holy of holies, and there appears in the presence of God, to engage in the last acts of His ministration in behalf of men — to perform the work of investigative judgment, **and to make an atonement for all who are shown to be entitled to its benefits.** (GC p.480)

And what of Froom's claims that Christ is merely administering the "benefits" of a completed atonement? Hear the truth from God's messenger:

**It is those who by faith follow Jesus in the great work of atonement, who receive the benefits of His mediation in their behalf; while those who reject the light which brings to view this work of ministration, are not benefited thereby.**(GC p.430)

So it can be seen that Dr Froom's claim of benefits being provided from a completed earthly atonement is complete nonsense. What does inspiration say Christ is doing? He is **'pleading his blood before the Father in behalf of sinners'.** Whether or not we receive the benefits of His mediation during this final phase of the atonement, is up to us. Who will NOT receive the benefits? **"Those who reject the light which brings to view this work of ministration."**

Do the authors of QOD reject this light? They certainly do, while taking upon themselves the awesome responsibility of interpreting the Spirit of Prophecy. Just listen to them:-

When therefore one hears an Adventist say, or reads in Adventist literature, even in the writings of Ellen G. White, that Christ is making atonement now, it should be understood that we mean simply that Christ is now making application of the benefits of the sacrificial atonement He made on the cross.(QOD pp. 354,355)

No wonder no one had the courage to append his signature to this specious document! No wonder Elder Andreasen described QOD as an attempt to lessen and destroy confidence in the Spirit of Prophecy and establish a "new theology"! - (See Letters to the Churches No 3.)

No wonder Dr Wilkinson claimed it was **a dagger aimed at the heart of Adventism!** What then, would he have said about Movement of Destiny?

*1. Arianism:  A belief pertaining to Arius of Alexandria in the fourth century who held Christ to be a super-angelic being.

That there is one Lord Jesus Christ, the Son of the Eternal Father, the one by whom God created all things, and by whom they do consist; that He took on Him the nature of the seed of Abraham for the redemption of our fallen race; that He dwelt among men, full of grace and truth, lived our example, died our sacrifice, and was raised for our justification.

He ascended on high to be our only mediator in the sanctuary in Heaven, where, with His own blood, He makes atonement for our sins; which atonement so far from being made on the cross, which was by the offering of the sacrifice is the very last portion of His work as priest according to the example of the Levitical priesthood, which fore-shadowed and prefigured the ministry of our Lord in Heaven. See Lev. 16; Heb. 8:4,5; 9:6,7; etc.

— Declaration of Fundamental Principles Taught and Practiced by The Seventh-day Adventists, 1872. Principle No. 2.

# CHAPTER 12

# FALSE CLAIMS
# AND TRICKERY

---

The history of apostasy in the Christian Church testifies to the fact that the introduction of heresies is a gradual process. Sometimes they are introduced as acceptable alternatives as in the case of Constantine's introduction of Sunday as a holy day. Others are introduced as new light on previously held views that eventually end up as supposed corrections to that view. Still others gain a foothold on the basis that the church has held them all along, but somehow they have been forgotten. None of the heresies gain instant widespread acceptance, simply because it takes time for a generation of believers to pass away.

Such methods to achieve change are being repeated in Seventh-day Adventism today. Just listen to Dr Froom:

And in addition to the complete Deity of Christ, Adventists had long been emphasizing the completed Act of Atonement on the Cross, with our High Priest applying its wondrous benefits through His heavenly ministry. This was now our standard and general teaching — for decades before the time of the interviews. And as stated, this was affirmed and buttressed by the uniform baptismal certificate, with its covenant and vows of 1941 required of all candidates for membership in the Seventh-day Adventist Church. (MOD p.482)

Let us examine this statement and its implications. Firstly, a truth is stated — Adventists

had long been emphasizing the complete deity of
Christ, (meaning that we were not Arian) but it
is coupled to an untruth - that we had long
accepted the notion of a completed act of
atonement at the cross and that Christ is now
merely applying the benefits of that act.

Secondly, we are told that this had been our
standard teaching for "decades" prior to the
Evangelical interviews commenced in 1955, (but
meaning, at least since 1935).

Thirdly, it was a requirement of belief for
all baptismal candidates since 1941.

Now let us test the credibility of Froom's
statements. We will go back to the year 1952,
only three years prior to the Evangelical
interviews, when the editor of Review & Herald,
F.D. Nichol, published his ministerial handbook,
Answers to Objections. Speaking of some objections to our doctrines over which some leave the
Adventist Church he observes on page 751:

He [the ex-Adventist] speaks militantly of
the "finished work of Christ on the cross".

Nichol then goes to some pains to show that
such a position is devoid of logic:

Of those who charge us with teaching strange
doctrines because we believe that Christ's
work of atonement for sin was begun rather
than completed on Calvary we ask the question
"If a complete and final atonement was made
on the cross for all sins, then will not all
be saved?" for Paul says that 'He died for
all'.

Are we to understand you as being universal-
ists? 'No', you say, 'not all men will be
saved.' Well then, are we to understand that
you hold that Christ made complete atonement

on the cross for only a limited few, and that
His sacrifice was not world embracing, but
only partial? That would be predestination in
its worst form. (ATO 1952 p.408)

Note the time--just three years prior to the
evangelical meetings--not "decades"! But the
editor of the Review and Herald was by no means
the only one of our leaders to believe in a
continuing atonement. Other books written and/or
circulating during the decades 1935-1955 which
upheld Christ's continuing work of atonement
come to mind:

| | |
|---|---|
| W.H.Branson's | Drama of the Ages |
| F.C. Gilbert's | Messiah in His Sanctuary |
| C.H. Watson's | Atoning Work of Christ |
| M.L. Andreasen's | The Sanctuary Service |
| and | The Epistle to the Hebrews |

On the other hand, we know of no books published by Adventism that taught a 'completed
atonement' prior to the publication of Questions
On Doctrine. We have noted how, in the 1949
revision of Bible Readings the 'repugnant'
reference to Christ's 'sinful fallen nature' had
been deleted.   Yet, no attempt to revise our
belief on the heavenly atonement was made.   We
quote from the 1951 edition published by Review
& Herald:
> In the service of the heavenly sanctuary
> there is but one sacrifice; and but one
> atonement, or cleansing of the heavenly
> sanctuary, can be made, which must take place
> at the time assigned of God for it. (Bible
> Readings 1951 p.205)
> As the atonement day of the former dispen-
> sation was really a day of judgment, so the
> atonement work of Christ will include the

investigation of the cases of His people prior to His coming the second time to receive them unto Himself. (Ibid p.207)

So much for Froom's "standard and general teaching for <u>decades</u> before the interviews"! But what about his assertion that the "completed atonement" was "affirmed and buttressed by the Baptismal certificate of 1941"? Let's take a careful look at Baptismal Vow No 2:

Do you accept the death of Jesus Christ on Calvary as an atoning sacrifice for the sins of men and believe that through faith in His shed blood, men are saved from sin and its penalty? (Church Manual 1951 Edition)

Can an honest person agree with Froom's contention that this vow supports a 'Completed Act of Atonement on the Cross'? This vow describes Christ's death as an "atoning sacrifice" just as we would describe the sacrifice in the typical earthly service. Interestingly, this vow also states that we are saved "through faith in His shed blood", which is backed up by traditional Adventist teaching and the Spirit of Prophecy.

Speaking of the heavenly sanctuary, Mrs White writes:

The ark that enshrines the tables of the law is covered with the mercy-seat before which Christ pleads His blood in the sinner's behalf. This is represented as the union of justice and mercy in the plan of redemption. (<u>Great Controversy</u> p.415)

And what of the men who formulated this baptismal statement? Did they intend it to uphold Froom's contention that it "confirmed and buttressed" a complete atonement? The committee which formulated the baptismal vow consisted of thirteen men under the chairmanship of W.H. Branson, some of whom were:

J L McElhany,            G.C. President
W G Turner,           G.C. Vice—President
L E Froom,   Secretary of Ministerial Association
R A Anderson,     Associate Ministerial Secretary
D E Rebok, President of SDA Theological Seminary

(D E Rebok is credited with the actual altera- tion of Bible Readings on the "nature of Christ" under the direction of R A Anderson)

Well, we probably know what Froom and Anderson had in mind as to the meaning behind the wording of the vow, because of their later obvious desire to alter our sanctuary belief to please Barnhouse. But what of Elder Branson, who was appointed the chairman of the committee? In his book, Drama of the Ages, Branson says:

> In the heavenly (Sanctuary) the blood of Jesus is actually presented as a sacrificial atonement for the sins of the people. In the earthly sanctuary the services were performed by men. In the heavenly, Christ is the mini- ster, and daily pleads the merits of His own blood in behalf of repentant sinners.(p.257)

Furthermore, Branson had upheld Nichol's teaching of a continuing atonement when he wrote the Foreword to Answers to Objections. In it, Branson made known his attitude to Adventist doctrine:

> Throughout their entire history, Seventh-day Adventists have stood for certain distinct doctrines, some of which differ rather sharply from the teachings of other Christian

bodies.    Because of our insistence upon the
scriptural   authenticity   of   these   unpopular
teachings,  we  have  naturally  found  it  frequently  necessary  to  defend  our  positions
against those who would by careless or faulty
interpretation  seek  to  sweep  away  the  distinctive tenets of our faith.

How awesomely significant then, to realize in
retrospect,    that    at    least    one    member    of
Branson's  committee  had  knowingly  helped  to
formulate  a  baptismal  vow  that  [to  his  way  of
thinking] could be interpreted later to uphold a
completed  atonement!      Significantly,  although
holding  the  position  of  ministerial  secretary
and editor of the Ministry from 1941–1950, Froom
kept  his  interpretation  and  views  of  an  emascu-
lated  atonement  out  of  print  until  such  time  as
a  sympathetic  president  ascended  the  throne  in
Washington.    One  can  only  speculate  as  to  how
many  more  cuckoo's  eggs  are  nestling  snugly  in
the    "fundamental"    jargon    of    Seventh-day
Adventism!

# Chapter 13

# CZARDOM? KINGDOM?
## or POPEDOM?

---

We have seen how error rides smugly on the back of truth. But the converse is not possible, for truth cannot be attracted to error. It is therefore evident that any cause which relies on concealment, trickery and lies, or any other subterfuge to get its message across, must of necessity be a dishonest cause. This fact alone should discount any doctrinal conclusions drawn from dishonest arguments and propositions as found in Questions On Doctrine and Movement Of Destiny.

But sadly, these books are now looked upon by the majority of administrators and leaders in the SDA church in Australasia as doctrinally authoritative. Those who point out the twin errors of Christ's limited humanity and His limited atonement are penalised by an administration which is bent on carrying out an undertaking given to Barnhouse to enforce the new stand. This is not altogether surprising when we remember that both books were published with the blessings of the contemporary G.C. presidents* 1. and promoted vigorously by the vast resources of the church.

Before this deplorable dilemma can be resolved, it is essential that we understand the political side of the equation. It is essential to discover how an organization which was formed to preach the three angels' messages has now become counter-productive to the very aims which brought it into existence. Why is it that the call to "come out of Babylon" has been replaced by demands to conform to Babylon? Why is it, that instead of being a separate people, we now find ourselves in bed with Babylon's daughters - the popular Evangelicals?

Only with a proper understanding of the mechanism which has assisted this unholy union will the church be able to return to its God-given task of preaching the third angel's message and be in a position to repel future attempts at seduction. In other words, it is vital that we learn from history in order that we may profit by our mistakes. It is not generally known that organisation and religious liberty were issues around the time of the 1888 meetings. Just prior to the commencement of the General Conference meetings at Battle Creek, 1901 Mrs White had declared that there must be:

an entire new organisation and to have a Committee that shall take in not merely half a dozen that is to be a ruling and controlling power ... To have this Conference pass on and close up as the Conferences have done, with the same manipulating, with the very same tone, and the same order - God forbid! ...This thing has been continued for the last fifteen years or more, and God calls for a change...(quoted by Jones in a letter to Daniells, 26th Jan. 1906)

This makes it plain that Mrs White was objecting to an organisation that had allowed a few men to "manipulate" our work for a period extending back prior to the 1888 conference. She continued:

From the light that I have... There was a narrow compass here; there within that narrow compass is a king-like, a kingly ruling power. God means what He says, 'I want a change here!' (Ibid)

It was this 'kingly' power which had prevented our leaders from humbling their hearts and had thwarted the Holy Spirit's attempts to bless our church with the latter rain. At the 1893 General Conference in Battle Creek, Elder A.T. Jones had drawn such a spontaneous confession from the delegates while lecturing on the third angel's message:

Now brethren, when did that message of the righteousness of Christ begin with us as a people? [One or two in the audience: "Three or four years ago"] ...Yes, four. Where was it? [Congregation: "Minneapolis"] What then did the brethren reject at Minneapolis? The Loud Cry ...They rejected the latter rain — the loud cry of the third angel's message. (G.C. Bulletin 1893 p.183)

It seems that A.T. Jones soon incurred the displeasure of President Daniells who had sought to circumscribe his activities during his term at Battle Creek Sanitarium as Bible instructor. But problems soon arose as Daniells saw fit to take part in secret meetings with others of the Sanitarium staff to which Jones was not invited.

During an address at a regular monthly meeting of the Sanitarium family held on March 4, 1906, Jones commented at some length on the meetings and said, "Whatsoever is not as open as the day is of the methods of Satan."* 2.

Jones then read to the meeting most of a letter which he had written to Daniells a few weeks earlier, on 26th January. In the main, it had recounted the history of the re-organisation of the General Conference in 1901, and the subsequent return in 1903 of the conference to its

former bureaucracy.*   He reminded Daniells that
the re-organisation in 1901 was:

> ...the call away from a centralized order of
> things in which ...a few men held the ruling
> and directing power to an organization in
> which all the people as individuals should
> have a part, with God, in Christ, by the Holy
> Spirit as the unifying and directing power."

It was with this understanding that a new
constitution was adopted and, "the monarchy was
swept away completely."   This was in harmony
with Mrs White's wishes.  Said she:

> We want to understand that there are no gods
> in our Conference.  There are to be no kings
> here and no kings in any conference that is
> formed, 'all ye are brethren'. (quoted in
> Jones letter to Daniells)

So it is quite evident that the former organisation had degenerated into a bureaucratic
power led by presidents. Mrs White called it a
"kingly power". This had now changed. It was
replaced by a committee as described by Jones:

> Under this (new) constitution the General
> Conference Committee was composed of a large
> number of men, with power to organise itself
> by choosing a chairman, etc. No president of
> the General Conference was chosen; nor was
> any provided for. The presidency of the
> General Conference was eliminated to escape a
> centralized power, a one-man power, a king-
> ship, a monarchy. (Ibid)

But the General Conference did not remain
without a president for long. Like Israel of old
there was a clamour for "kingly" leaders. Let
Jones take up the story as he castigates

Daniells for disobeying the wishes of God by violating the newly-formed constitution (just two years on from 1901).

"...A few men ...without any kind of authority, but directly against the plain words of the constitution, took it absolutely upon themselves to elect you president, and Brother Prescott vice-president of the General Conference. And that there never was in this universe a clearer piece of usurpation of position, power, and authority.

You two were, then, of right, just as much president and vice-president of Timbuktu as you were of the Seventh-day Adventist General Conference." (Ibid)

The strength of this rebuke to the two top officers of the church should not be lost upon readers.* Jones then outlines the actions taken by Daniells and his supporters to give the usurpation an air of legitimacy:

4.

"A new constitution was framed to fit and to uphold usurpation." (Ibid)

This, Jones saw as, "A Czardom" ..."which has since gone steadily forward," and he went on to back up his view with the feelings of some men of experience within the denomination:

"...there has never been such a one-man power, such a centralized despotism, so much of papacy...! And as a part of this bureaucracy, there is of all the incongruous things ever heard of, a Religious Liberty Bureau - a contradiction in terms." (Ibid)

And now for Jones' summation of the situation:

**The Seventh-day Adventist denomination is more like the Catholic Church than is any other Protestant church in the world.*** (Ibid)

5.

[For reproduction of Jones' historic letter, see Appendix]
And so within the Seventh-day Adventist church was re-installed an instrument of "papal-like, kingly" authority, the basic structure of which remains in place to this day. This is not to infer that all succeeding presidents have taken advantage of the "kingly" authority. But some have used it to the peril of our church; either intentionally or by manipulation, a few men have usurped a position comparable to the Vatican Curia, taking upon themselves the responsibility of redefining our church doctrines.

*1. As previously noted, Pastor Pierson later repudiated his Foreword to <u>Movement of Destiny</u>.

*2. Jones enunciated a principle which does not appear to be understood by some present-day administrators of the S.D.A. Church, e.g. the secrecy of board-room meetings.

*3. Jones quotes from the Standard Dictionary:
"A bureaucracy is sure to think that its duty is to augment official power, official business, or official numbers, rather than to leave free the energies of mankind."
This could explain the decretive manner in which the South Pacific Division recently foisted a Babylonian--like hymnbook and a gallows-like logo upon our church.

*4. Neither was this rebuke lost upon Daniells. Many consider that as a result of such outspoken rebukes, Daniells virtually hounded Jones out of the Church. But it seems that in later life, Daniells repented of his attitude towards Jones and acknowledged that, "Jones was right and I was wrong". (Source: Pr G. Burnside, following conversation with Meade Mc Guire in USA, 1946)

*5. Let us remind the reader that this is Jones describing the S.D.A. organisation of 1906. Any similarity of Jones' description to conditions today is entirely providential and warrants close examination.

# CHAPTER 14

# THE ATONEMENT - COMPLETED
## OR UNCOMPLETED?
# WHO CARES?

---

Recently the author was discussing Adventism's latest pronouncement - Seventh-day Adventists Believe... with a retired minister. The observation was made that President N C Wilson and the General Conference* were still pushing the heresy of a completed atonement and cited the following:

1.

> The atonement, or reconciliation, was completed on the cross as foreshadowed by the sacrifices, and the penitent believer can trust in this finished work of our Lord. (Seventh-day Adventists Believe... p.315)

Imagine the author's surprise to learn that this minister, who to the best of the author's knowledge is a firm believer in our sanctuary message, could see nothing wrong with such a statement.*

2.

A similar experience took place a few days later while talking to a very respected evangelist whose faith in our sanctuary and other historic messages seems undiminished. He could see nothing wrong with the claims of Questions On Doctrine and Movement of Destiny, that Christ is now "administering the benefits of a completed atonement at the cross". Both men felt that the author was reading an unwarranted intent into a perfectly innocent statement.

But let it ever be remembered that the overriding purpose of QOD was to convince Chris-

tendom that we believed in Christ's completed
work of atonement [and by implication, salva-
tion] in order to escape the stigma of cultism.
Having satisfied Barnhouse and Martin on this
point, these men then ridiculed our claim that
Christ was carrying on a further work in the
heavenly sanctuary as being illogical.  Said
Barnhouse:
> "...any effort to establish it [Christ's
> heavenly ministry] is stale, flat and unprof-
> itable". (<u>Eternity</u>, Sep.1956)

And again:
> ...the latter doctrine (investigative judg-
> ment), to me, is the most colossal, face-
> -saving phenomenon in religious history..!
> (Ibid)

An attempt to overcome such logical criticism
is currently being manifested in the South
Pacific Division where ministers are teaching
that the "pre-advent judgment", [the preferred
term for the investigative judgment]*refers to
God's judgment i.e. it is God who is being
judged in order that the universe should see the
justice of God in His dealings with Satan.
While preaching at the Avondale Memorial
church, Pastor Geoff Youlden of the South
Pacific Division Media Centre, claimed that in
the pre-Advent judgment, "God is up for judgment" and that "God is in the hotseat". When the
author later pointed out to him that this is an
echo of Fordian teaching,* he claimed that he
knew nothing of what Ford believes or teaches!
Such a claim is all the more astounding when it
is realised that Youlden studied under Ford at
Avondale College.  (Sermon "The Gospel and the
Judgment" 20th August, 1988)  Such teaching
appears to retain belief in the investigative

judgment, while shifting its emphasis on to God's shoulders. Thus the urgency of the first angel's message of Rev. 14 which is an urgent call for personal preparedness, is effectively muted.

This view is not only comparatively new to Adventism but is contrary to the Spirit of Prophecy:

The act of Christ in dying for the salvation of man would not only make heaven accessible to men, but before all the universe it would justify God and His Son in their dealing with the rebellion of Satan.(Patriarchs & Prophets p.69) (See Appendix for chapter 25)

The authority of the Spirit of Prophecy is upheld in the S.D.A. Bible Commentary. Here it is clearly acknowledged that God's method of dealing with sin has been eternally vindicated before the universe:

The supreme demonstration was made by the incarnation, life and death of God's own Son. God now stood wholly vindicated before the universe ...Thus the charges of Satan were refuted and the peace of the universe was made eternally sure. God's character had been vindicated before the universe. (See Patriarchs & Prophets pp.68,69), (S.D.A. Bible Commentary Vol 6, p.508)

There is no doubt that many Adventists are quite naive in accepting deceptive pronouncements which are aimed at destroying Biblical Adventist positions. If such statements should come with the blessings of presidents and others who have attained influential positions, it becomes difficult to accept that such statements are misleading. Instead, some strive to inter-

pret these statements to harmonize with traditional Adventist beliefs. **This is the genius of
Satan's chicanery, for while trusting souls are
silently consenting, heretics are energetically
exploiting this dual state of the art.**

Dr Desmond Ford, ex-minister of the S.D.A.
church and still a member of Pacific Union College church, exploits the "finished atonement"
concept to explain his evangelical view of a
term used almost exclusively by Adventists -
"Everlasting Gospel".   In his magazine, Good
News Australia, (Aug.1988), Ford writes under
the heading "Meditation upon the Everlasting
Gospel".  He says:

> Thus in every place where Paul mentions 'the
> righteousness of faith, he means not sancti-
> fication, but that justification which is
> based on the finished atonement'. (p.2)

Notice that his conclusions on sanctification
and justification are based on a "finished
atonement".

Even being a credentialed minister of the SDA
church does not hinder Pastor Vern Heise from
expressing his views in Ford's Good News
Australia.  Naturally, they are compatible with
Ford's evangelical-type Gospel.  In an article
"Have you been to church at Antioch?", Heise
takes a tilt at religious "groups that feel that
they are 'sole custodians of truth'". Of course,
being a veteran minister past retiring age, he
would be very aware that the S.D.A. Church is
the "sole custodian" of the sanctuary truth with
its judgment-hour message.  Heise tells us that:

> There were those in Jerusalem that wanted to
> make Christianity hard work. They were enjoy-
> ing their masochism - their self-imposed pen-
> ances.  They were  like some  today who will

perform their religion even if it kills them!
(GNA Sep. 1988)

Then comes the punch line to which his whole
article has been targeted:
On the other hand, the church in Antioch rejoiced in and celebrated the finished work of
Christ. (Ibid)

Yes, that is how the "finished work of our
Lord" (Seventh-day Adventists Believe...) is
being interpreted from within our church -
shades of Barnhouse who sees our belief in
Christ's heavenly atoning ministry as "stale,
flat and unprofitable" and the keeping of the
Sabbath as legalistic.(a "self-imposed penance"?
"Performing their religion even if it kills
them"?)
May we remind the reader of Elder F D
Nichol's words quoted back in chapter 12:
**..The ex-Adventist) speaks militantly of the
finished work of Christ on the cross.** (ATO
p.751)

Now, over thirty-five years on, **it is a
credentialed, ordained minister of the Seventh-
day Adventist church who so speaks!** And who
does he now have to back him? Well, according
to Seventh-day Adventists Believe..." he could
quote the Ministerial Association, who have the
authorisation and encouragement of President
Neal C Wilson and the other officers of the
General Conference.
But worse is to come. The Ministerial Association tells us that Seventh-day Adventists
Believe... is a Biblical exposition of the
twenty-seven "Fundamental Beliefs of Seventh-day
Adventists". (p.IV and cover title) Yet all the

while, recent converts to our church and young people particularly, are being brainwashed with the Evangelical interpretation of a make-believe brother/Saviour who finished His work at Calvary.

To the carnal mind, a bargain in cheap grace or salvation in sin, is very appealing. Qualms of conscience can be assuaged by deductive reasoning based on new and erroneous positions touted by official publications of the S.D.A. church. It goes something like this:

Because Jesus came to this earth with the nature of unfallen Adam, He did not inherit the sinful tendencies that I received from my parents, and therefore, He had an advantage over me and He does not expect me to follow Him as my example.

And because He completed His atoning work of salvation at the cross, there is no need for a later investigative judgment in heaven. If I try to keep His commandments, I am rejecting Christ's victory over sin on my behalf and I am actually committing the sin of trying to save myself by my own works.

Perhaps in the cold light of logic, we should be grateful to the General Conference for showing us in Seventh-day Adventists Believe... that they are unable to clearly interpret their Fundamental Belief No. 23, as enunciated at Dallas. Just look at this pathetic effort to portray the earthly sacrifice as the atonement in an attempt to make their "completed atonement" at the cross appear credible:

The application of the atoning blood during the mediatorial ministry of the priest was also seen as a form of atonement" Lev.4:35. (Seventh-day Adventists Believe... p.315)

"A form of atonement?"   What nonsense!   It
was a crucial part of the atonement!

But lo and behold!   These equivocators are
caught in the trap of their own making and go on
to contradict their previous statement of "the
finished work".   In defiance of Barnhouse's and
Ford's logic, they have to justify Christ's
further ministry in heaven. They say:

Christ's priestly ministry provides for the
sinner's forgiveness and reconciliation to
God. Heb. 7:25  (Ibid p.317)

And again:

The heavenly sanctuary is the great command
centre where Christ conducts His priestly
ministry for our salvation. (Ibid p.316)

And yet, on the previous page, we have been
told that "the atonement or reconciliation was
completed on the cross"! (Ibid 315) Such is the
dilemma into which people arrive when they endeavour to produce a book on Adventist beliefs
that has something for everyone.*  And if this   5.
dose of double-talk has not sufficiently confused the meaning of Fundamental 23, here is
some more, as we read:

The issue [investigative judgment] is with
God and the universe, not between God and the
true child. (Ibid p.326)

In the light of such enchanting statements,
the instruction given by God's messenger takes
on a new urgency for Seventh-day Adventists
today:

We are individually to be judged according to
the deeds done in the body.  In the typical
service, when the work of atonement was performed by the high priest in the most holy
place of the earthly sanctuary,  the people

were required to afflict their souls before
God, and confess their sins, that they might
be atoned for and blotted out.  Will any less
be required of us in this anti-typical day of
atonement, when Christ in the sanctuary above
is pleading in behalf of His people, and the
final irrevocable decision is to be pronounced upon every case?...
We must no longer remain upon enchanted
ground.  We are fast approaching the close of
probation...Let the church arise, and repent
of her backslidings before God.  Let the
watchmen awake and give the trumpet a certain
sound.  It is a definite warning that we have
to proclaim.  God commands His servants 'Cry
aloud, spare not, lift up thy voice like a
trumpet, and shew my people their transgression, and the house of Jacob their
sins.(Isa. 58:1), (<u>1 Selected Messages</u> pp.
125,126)

So, just how important is it that Seventh-day
Adventists resist the teaching of a completed
atonement?  Let us hear from the Church's pro-
claimed authority on the sanctuary:
**No Adventist can believe in a final atonement
on the cross and remain an Adventist.**
(Andreasen, <u>Letters to the Churches</u> titled
"The Living Witness" p.2 as reprinted by LMN
Publishing, 1988)

The truth of this statement is supported by
the Spirit of Prophecy:
The scripture which above all others had been
both the foundation and central pillar of the
Advent faith was the declaration "Unto two
thousand and three hundred days; then shall
the sanctuary be cleansed.  Daniel 8:14 (<u>The</u>

Story of Redemption p.375)

When Christ entered the most holy place of
the heavenly sanctuary to perform the closing
work of the atonement, He committed to His
servants the last message of mercy to be
given to the world.   Such is the warning of
the third angel of Revelation 14. (Ibid
p.379)

*1.Under the heading "We Gratefully Acknowledge..", we read:
"With the authorization and encouragment of President
Neal C Wilson and the other officers of the General
Conference of Seventh-day Adventists, the Ministerial
Association has undertaken to prepare this volume to
furnish reliable information of beliefs of our church."
(S.D.As Believe... p.v)

*2.The reader will notice that this statement not only
repeats Froom's error of a completed atonement, but
incorrectly implies that this was foreshadowed by the
earthly sacrifices, and comes perilously close to
satisfying the Evangelicals' demands that a Christian
must believe in Christ's completed work of salvation.

*3.In S.D.As Believe... p. 317, the investigative judgment
is referred to as the "pre-millenial judgment" and
"pre-Advent judgment".

*4.Ford wrote in Australian Signs of the Times, 24 June 1957
under the heading, "Will Believers and Their Sins Come to
Judgment?": "God has placed himself on trial before the
universe."

*5 Many consider the latest statement of Fundamental Beliefs
to be a consensus statement.  This was openly claimed by
Pastor Rex Moe at a special business meeting of the
Avondale Memorial Church (27 Sep. 1987) in his attempt to
prove that various interpretations of our Fundamentals
are allowed. Now, in Seventh-day Adventists Believe...,
we have the farcical situation of a consensus interpretation of a consensus statement!

Elder A F Ballenger was once one of our leading evangelists, and won many souls to the truth. Eventually he was dismissed from the church because of theological differences, and, as one would say, "of all things", the heresy for which he was dismissed is the very doctrine now being forced upon us, teaching that the atonement was made on the cross!

In commenting on his dismissal Mrs White said: "... [his] proofs are not reliable. If received they would destroy the faith of God's people in the truth that has made us what we are."

"... It was under the guidance of the Holy Spirit that the presentations of the sanctuary question were given ... Another and still another, will arise and bring in supposed great light, and make their assertions. But we stand by the old landmarks ..." (1SM 161–162)

                    — M L Andreasen on the Atonement
          (Letters to the Churches, Jan 19, 1958).

# Chapter 15

# TARGET AUSTRALIA

It was well-nigh impossible for heresy to gain a permanent foothold while God's messenger, Mrs E G White was alive. Her influence survived her death and the work prospered in proportion to the number of her dwindling contemporaries.

Particularly was this so in Australasia, where Mrs White had established the Avondale School for Christian workers (now known as Avondale College) according to the blueprint. This model of Christian education was eventually to make its presence felt as its missionaries not only encompassed Australasia, but they were eventually to take a prominent part in speeding the advance of the everlasting gospel around the world.

They had no illusions as to the messages contained in the everlasting gospel and they did not deem it advisable to attend colleges of "higher" learning to discover that message. They called their brothers out of Babylon into God's remnant church, that they too might catch a vision of a judgment-bound world on the brink of eternity. They were not ashamed of this "gospel of Christ" with His atoning role as ministering High Priest in the heavenly sanctuary.

If, and when Satan tried to gain an heretical foothold within the church, such efforts were stoutly and ably resisted. One such attempt was made in the late 'twenties through the person of one of Australasia's capable leaders, Pastor W.W. Fletcher. Some say that he had been sidetracked by Elder L.R. Conradi of Europe, on our sanctuary message and on the Spirit of Prophecy.

Let it be stated here, that unlike some later and contemporary heretics, Pr Fletcher presented his propositions honestly by acknowledging that he believed differently to historic Adventism.

A sub-committee was appointed early in 1930 to study Fletcher's propositions by the then Australasian Union Conference of which Pastor W. G.Turner was president. Their report which rejected Fletcher's views, was forwarded to the General Conference where another committee had been formed to counsel with Fletcher. The chairman of that committee, Pastor Montgomery, wrote to the Australasian Union thanking them for the sub-committee's work and conclusions. He said:

We feel that this statement is both tenable and adequate to prove the error of the views held by Brother Fletcher.

In the light of present heresies, it is interesting to note one of the highlights of the sub-committee's statements:

If sin was cancelled at the cross, there is no need for a scapegoat. The typical service however, provided one, which is proof that the sin was not cancelled at the altar of burnt offering, which is the equivalent of the cross. The sin was finally atoned for, not at the cross, but in the true tabernacle in heaven before the "ark of the testament", which John saw in vision. (p.5)

The late Pastor A.W. Anderson was asked to prepare a paper on Fletcher's attitude to our sanctuary doctrine. This was circulated with the committee's report. In it he correctly observed:

On the reconciliation (atonement), "That this reconciliation was not completed on the cross is evident from the fact that it was the work

of a high priest to make reconciliation. When
He was on earth, He was not a priest". (See
Heb. 8:4)
"If reconciliation was completed on the
cross, then when Christ entered the heavenly
sanctuary with His own blood and became our
High Priest, His work as a priest was already
completed."
The concluding paragraph states:
"After a careful re-examination of the ninety
passages of scripture in which the words
'atonement' and 'reconciliation' occur, I am
more profoundly convinced than ever that W.W.
Fletcher is wrong, and the denominational
teaching on the cleansing of the sanctuary is
right."
(It should be noted that one of the men on
the General Conference Committee which commended
their Australasian brethren for their defence of
a continuing atonement in the heavenly sanctuary
was none other than L.E. Froom!)

God signally blessed the efforts of His
hard-working, dedicated servants and time came
when the homelands of Australia and New Zealand
attained one of the highest percentages of
Adventists in the world. But things were to
change. Satan had targeted this hard-won bastion
of truth for one of his most amazingly successful attacks against God's remnant church. He was
to succeed eventually in reversing the role of
the "blueprint" missionary college to that of a
veritable brooder of heresy, with the inevitable
result of bringing the advance of the third
angel of Revelation 14 to a virtual standstill
in Australia and New Zealand.
This dramatic change is revealed in the
statistical reports published annually in the

Australasian Record. For instance, the report for the year ending June 1972, shows a peak membership gain of approximately 1,023 in the two homeland Unions. This was achieved with the help of 235 ordained ministers. Within ten years (1982) the annual gain had dropped to 448 souls but it took 52 more ministers (287) to achieve this dismal result. The total tithe received in the homelands in 1982 was $18,577,755 which means that for each member increase, it cost $41,468 of tithe against $4,697 for each member increase back in 1972. During the year ending 1984, the Trans-Australian Union Conference actually suffered a membership loss of 166 members!

How could such a catastrophe come about? We must hark back to those fateful years of the early 'fifties when Vice-president Figuhr and his boys of the Washington club were smarting under the stigma of cultism. When Elder Figuhr came to Australia shortly before his election to the General Conference presidency, he used his fist to emphasize the direction in which he believed authority should travel:

"Representation comes up," he said, "but direction comes down."

At that same gathering in Melbourne, he also gave our workers an insight into the character- istics of leaders best-qualified to keep that authority moving in the desired direction. He is reported to have spoken along these lines:

When a man's name is brought up for nomina- tion to leadership, it is not his spiritual or doctrinal standing that is to be ques- tioned, or even his administrative capabil- ities. No, it is his ability to get on well with his fellows and maintain harmony that should be of paramount consideration.

According to the worker reporting this revelation, this was a rather startling departure
from accepted ideals and practice. There was no
doubt in the worker's mind that Figuhr was
speaking about pliable middle-of-the-road men*      1.
Many years later, Australian Adventists were to
see the baleful results of the implementation of
this unscriptural policy.

In the year 1957, our zealous Dr Froom came
to Australasia, promoting his book Prophetic
Faith of Our Fathers and the forthcoming book
Questions On Doctrine. We are told that he took
the opportunity to prepare our ministry for the
great leap "forward" that would be expected to
follow our new understanding of righteousness by
faith. He introduced them to the mysteries of
Christ's "vicarious human nature" and the
wonders of His "completed atonement".*              2.

By the end of the same year, Dr Edward
Heppenstall of the Washington Seminary had
arrived at Avondale College to take part in a
lengthy extension school for ministers. After a
lapse of over thirty years, recollections of all
that transpired in his lectures are growing dim.
But certain shock statements have left their
mark. One student recalls how Heppenstall told
them that there is only one covenant. When asked
how such a statement can be reconciled with
Adventists' two-covenant position as outlined in
Patriarchs & Prophets,* he is reported to have    3.
replied smugly, "You don't".

Others recall how he frequently stressed the
need for ministers to emphasize the love of God
in their sermons, and left them with the feeling
that perhaps doctrines were not too important.
Yet another remembers how Heppenstall recited

his encounters with M.L. Andreasen whom he portrayed as a decided hindrance to the advancement
of Adventism!

Still others of his students claim that
Heppenstall prevented the then Division President, F.G. Clifford from sitting in on his
classes.   In hindsight, this is not surprising
as Clifford's reputation for doctrinal orthodoxy
had probably registered in Washington.  By some
accounts, there were three students who made
quite an impression, not only on Heppenstall,
but also on their colleagues.  It appears that
Heppenstall was very impressed by their receptive attitude to "new light". He warmly commended them and urged them to go abroad for
advanced study. Some dutifully followed his
advice and eventually all three achieved a
degree of notoriety among Adventists:  Desmond
Ford left the imprint of his name on apostate
Adventism, and his theology in Avondale College;
Walter R.L. Scragg achieved the honour while
president of the Euro-African Division, of over-
seeing the bestowal of the gold-plated medal on
the Pope;* and Lenil Moulds was fired from the     4.
Theological Department of Avondale College for
teaching heresy which he picked up while studying in a North American Adventist University.*    5.

So it was, that doubts on the competency of
those who worked out our historic doctrinal positions were planted in the minds of our workers
while the authority of leadership as interpreters of scripture and the Spirit of Prophecy was
established in the minds of many.  All that was
needed now was a pliable leadership, amenable to
the dictates of a Washington hierarchy.  But the
time was not yet.  President Clifford had a firm
grip of the reins. As Froom had seriously observed: *                                          6.

"We need more funerals to get Adventism up and going."

*1. While Figuhr was making his acceptance speech, after being elected G.C. President, he described himself as a "middle-of-the-road" man.

*2. Vicarious: deputed; acting for another; substituted (Collins)
    Vicariously: by substitution (Collins)
    If Christ took my human nature in place of me, what sort of nature does that leave me with?

*3. Pastor Mervyn Ball, a retired Australian evangelist, told the author how he quoted the Spirit of Prophecy. It counters a claim by L.E. Froom that the atonement had been completed at Calvary. Froom's only response was a stony silence. Apparently other workers felt too embarrassed to press the issue, a phenomenon that has shown up repeatedly in this Division's march toward apostasy.

*4. See Review & Herald Aug. 11, 1977 on Medal.

*5. Moulds is to be commended for showing a rare degree of honesty, in that, unlike some others at the College, he refused to conceal his new-found "faith" from the Administration.

*6. According to a tape of Mike Clute's interview, Froom would ring up Wilkinson on his birthday and express disappointment that he was still alive.

There are men among us in responsible positions who hold that the opinions of a few conceited philosophers so-called, are more to be trusted than the truth of the Bible, or the testimonies of the Holy Spirit. Such a faith as that of Paul, Peter, or John, is considered old-fashioned, and insufferable at the present day. It is pronounced absurd, mystical, and unworthy of an intelligent mind.

God has shown me that these men are Hazaels to prove a scourge to our people. They are wise above what is written. This unbelief of the very truths of God's word because human judgment cannot comprehend the mysteries of his work, is found in every district in all ranks of society. it is taught in most of our schools, and comes into the lessons of the nurseries.

E.G. White
— Testimonies, Volume 5, p.79.

# CHAPTER 16

# "WE NEED MORE FUNERALS"

---

While our Australasian workers were left pondering this twist to Adventist theology, Froom was busy back in Washington, defending and promoting <u>Questions On Doctrine</u> and anxiously counting the 'funerals'.

But they were slow in coming. Andreasen who was now an elderly man, just wouldn't go away and Wilkinson at eighty-five was aggravatingly healthy. And, there were those two troublesome missionaries, Elders Wieland and Short, who had submitted a paper, <u>1888 Re-Examined</u>, to the General conference. They had been sent back to their fields of labour in Africa after consenting to let the matter drop. But now, others had seen fit to circulate a number of copies of their paper and laymen were complaining about a cover-up.

The original response to Wieland and Short's paper by the Defense Committee, while not supportive, had been generally civil and understanding. It carried the signature of the Committee Chairman, W.E. Read, and was dated 4th Dec. 1951. It said: "The manuscript gives every evidence of earnest, diligent and painstaking effort..." but in September 1958, the two missionaries received a second report, from the officers of the General Conference - this time without signatures.

Not only had there been a change in presidents, (Figuhr had succeeded W.H. Branson) but there had been a decided reversal of tone and attitude. The General Conference stated:

After having checked  and examined the Spirit

of Prophecy sources and their use in the manuscript, it is evident that the authors have revealed considerable amateurishness in both research and use of facts. (p.47)

They concluded:

Had the authors succeeded in substantiating their charges, their work might have been worthy of serious consideration. (p.49)

In studying Wieland and Short's reply to such insults, one can only praise God for their Christian attitude. They were able to demonstrate that the General Conference's charges were unable to bear the test of careful analysis. To the careful reader, it would appear that the reckless charges of the leadership could be better applied to themselves. Nevertheless, Elders Wieland and Short were able to write:

Lastly, if anything in this analysis of 'appraisal' seems to be disrespectful, critical, or presumptuous to your dignity as the Lord's appointed leaders of His work, His 'anointed', we assure you that it is not so intended to be. Circumstances have required that we speak frankly. (Letter to Officers and Executive Committee of G.C. Oct. 1958)

These loyal workers were apparently resigned to letting the matter rest there, for in a letter addressed to the G.C. Secretary, W.R. Beach, Jan. 21 1959, they wrote:

"...We wish to state herewith our desire to leave this matter, to drop it henceforth and to continue as in the past to refrain from any agitation whatsoever or the pressing of our view upon the General Conference or the church ...We return to our missionfield, therefore with no desire to make an issue of our views there or elsewhere.

Here the matter could have rested, as far as Brethren Wieland and Short were concerned. They had delivered their message. But, in the providence of God, His messengers were not meant to remain silent. Things happened this way:

Being an employee of the General Conference, it is highly probable that L.E. Froom would be among those leaders who had complained, "that the manuscript (of Wieland and Short) revealed a very critical attitude concerning the leadership, the ministry, and the plane of work in God's cause" (G.C. "Further Appraisal of 1888 Re-Examined" p.2.)

This unfortunate attitude of many of our leaders was similar to that of the leaders in 1888 who rejected the Minneapolis message. They regarded the messengers, Waggoner and Jones, as young upstarts who were attacking the leadership of older and experienced men. These leaders were not willing to humble themselves by accepting the message lest they be seen as being reproved by God. Said Mrs White, while commenting on the Minneapolis situation:

They [the opposers] heard not, neither would they understand. Why? Lest they should be converted and have to acknowledge that all their ideas were not correct. This they were too proud to do, and therefore persisted in rejecting God's counsel and the light and evidence which had been given." (Ms 25, 1890, quoted in 1888 Re-Examined p.24)

As this rebuke to Wieland and Short came from the General Conference, (meaning its officers), the Church was once more doomed to wander in the wilderness and forego the outpouring of the

latter rain.   Once again its leaders had failed
to grasp the real meaning of righteousness by
faith in all its beauty and fullness.  But this
time the rejection would go even further.  The
church would eventually repudiate the "third
angel's message in verity."

I watched them tearing a building down,
    A gang of men in a busy town.
With a ho-heave-ho and a lusty yell
    They swung a beam and the sidewall fell.
I asked the foreman, "Are these men skilled
    And the men you'd hire if you had to build?"
He gave a laugh saying, "No indeed!
    Just common labour is all I need.
I can easily wreck in a day or two
    What builders have taken a year to do."

                                    - Anon
(Published in Review & Herald, January 7, 1954)

# CHAPTER 17

# AUSTRALASIA EMBRACES
# HERESY

In 1972 Dr Desmond Ford returned to Australia to resume his position as head of the Theology Department of Avondale college. Safely in his possession was a precious doctorate from Manchester University in England. Probably he carried with him something else of great import—a copy of Froom's recently released Movement of Destiny. Ford could scarcely believe his luck! Here was a book published by the Seventh-day Adventist Church, recommended by the president and vice-president of the General conference, to which he could appeal to support much of his popular evangelical view of the gospel, which was now even further clouded with shades of Plymouth Brethrenism.*

He had come a long way since taking the advice of Heppenstall back in 1957. Following Avondale College's affiliation with the Pacific Union College, he had returned to Avondale to complete his bachelor's degree and then, under sponsorship, had gone to America for postgraduate studies. By the early 'sixties, Dr Ford was appointed chairman of Avondale's Theology Department. It was not long before discerning ministers were noticing that ministerial graduates of the College were expressing some strange doctrinal beliefs.

Even more disturbing were Ford's expositions on the prophecies of Daniel 8 and 9 as published in papers like the Australasian Signs of the Times (See Signs of the Times, June-Oct. 1973). Although such articles impinged on Adventists'

1.

understanding of the sanctuary message with its investigative judgment, yet there seemed to be no counter from Division leadership. Protests from loyal ministers and laymen were not followed with the positive action that had been previously taken to combat heresy, as demonstrated in the handling of W.W. Fletcher and R. Greive. It seemed as if our leaders had been mesmerised!

It is not necessary to rehearse all the sorry tale of events leading up to an examination of Ford's doctrinal standing because they have been documented so well by other writers.* Neither is it desirable to divert too far from our pursuit of the methods used by leadership, firstly to cloak the dagger of apostasy and secondly, to follow the outworking of a form of governmental control described by Mrs White as "kingly power".

Suffice to say, Pastor R.R. Frame, then president of the Division, eventually and reluctantly agreed to a group of concerned ministers and laymen meeting with the Biblical Research Institute of Australasia, to put their case in the presence of Dr Ford. (See Appendix for names of participants) Two meetings were held, on the third and fourth of February, 1976. The irony of the situation is, that this institite had been established to examine "new light" and protect the church against the intrusion of heresy. In Ford's case, the BRI had made no attempt to examine his theology. Now the concerned brethren were virtually on trial as they presented the historic Adventist position on doctrines vital to the mission of Seventh-day Adventists.

As Ford defended his theology it became apparent to the older concerned men that he was expressing similar views to those of a previous chairman of Avondale College Bible Department, the late Pastor W.W. Fletcher. But there were two significant differences: Fletcher correctly admitted that he was out of step with the Spirit of Prophecy. He was eased out of the ministry. Ford attempted to cloak his heresies by expressing full confidence in Mrs White's writings.

Another difference was to be found in the attitude of the administrators. There had been no sympathy for Fletcher's popular evangelical views, while Ford obviously had the support of influential leaders. According to Dr R. Standish who participated in the meetings:

> The most heated speech of the day undoubtedly issued from the lips of one of the Conference presidents in defence of Dr Ford.* (Adventism Challenged, p.142)

Dr R.R. Standish gives credit to Pastors R. Stanley and A. Tolhurst for expressing reservations about what Ford was teaching, but unfortunately they did not press their point. We are told by another witness that Stanley's objections went over 'like a lead balloon':

> There was dead silence from the members of the BRI (Anchor No.7, p.2) (See Appendix for an eyewitness account.)

Among the Institute's findings, particularly in the area of the sanctuary, the age of the earth, and inspiration, they found:

1. That ...Dr Desmond Ford ably demonstrated that such stances as he takes which appear to diverge from what some senior men hold as 'Present Truth' can be justified by reference to majority positions taken by current Seventh-day Adventist authors and scholars.

2. The senior ministers (as represented by their speakers) were somewhat unaware of the movements in Adventist thought and style of doctrinal presentation in recent years, a fact which explains their reaction to some contemporary expositions. (As quoted in Adventism Challenged p.151)

In retrospect, it is plain to see that the Administration had abused the very purpose for which the Biblical Research Institute was named, for they found in favour of Ford on non-Biblical grounds, such grounds being what some scholars had written and taught!  Later, some in the Institute realised the terrible implication of being seen to accept doctrine on the authority of man, so the minutes were amended to add "the Bible and the Spirit of Prophecy" as a basis for Ford's stand!

This statement was later shown to be no more than a face-saving device as Ford was fired following Glacier View simply because he could not support his stand from Inspiration.

Further, their findings illustrate the tremendous inroads such books as Questions On Doctrine and Movement of Destiny had made into the thinking of Australasian leadership.  They admitted that there had been a "movement away" from our historic doctrines and then condemned our senior ministers for being unaware of the shift.

The Secretary of the Biblical Research Institute revealed to some extent the political opposition behind the grudging assent given the meeting, by "asserting that the whole concern was really simply a personal attack upon Dr Ford".* (Adventism Challenged p. 149) This disgraceful but revealing remark was immediately    4.

protested and then quickly withdrawn. (Ibid.)

So it was, that Ford and those who defended him all continued in their jobs, ostensibly to uphold and advance historic Bible-based Adventism, when in fact they had declared to the church that they upheld the "doctrines of men". To this very day, all of them who remain as active workers retain positions of prominence in administration or in educational fields.

*1. In the special edition of Ministry Oct. 1980, devoted to reporting the Glacier View meetings, is to be found a brief, but highly significant statement by Ford. Referring to his defence paper, he said:

" ...the task on which I was working was not a novel one, but one engaged upon by other men well known to us, such as W.W. Prescott and L.E. Froom."

As chairman of the Guiding committee for MOD, N.C. Wilson was later to find himself sitting in judgment of Ford, [as G.C. President] History has shown that he wore two hats!

The author heartily agrees that Ford was in the track of Froom but he is unaware of any reason to associate Froom with Prescott other than to attempt to invest Froom with some credibility.

*2. The author recommends the Standish Bros. book Adventism Challenged for an excellent account of the Australasian Division's march to apostasy. Obtainable from:

A.L.M.A. (M & L Harnell)
21 Tamworth Street,
ANNERLEY Qld 4103 Australia

*3. Following a heated attack by Pastor Rex Moe on the editor of Anchor magazine, (Avondale Memorial Church business meeting 27th Sept. 1987) Pastors G. Burnside and O.K. Anderson identified the Conference President who "heatedly" defended Ford, as Rex Moe.

*4.The Standish brothers do not reveal the identity of the
person making this statement. Other eye-witnesses have
identified him as the Secretary of the Institute and this
has been confirmed by R. Standish in conversation with
the author. This is an important point in establishing
the biased attitude of the BRI towards Ford. Other
witnesses claim that the Secretary spoke in much stronger
terms, accusing the concerned men of conducting a
"personal vendetta" against Ford.

# CHAPTER 18

# THE JEWEL IS PLUCKED

By the end of 1976, Pr. R.R. Frame had opted out of the controversy by resigning the presidency, handing over the reins of Division leadership to Pr. K. Parmenter. As Secretary of the Division at the time of the February BRI meetings, Parmenter had taken a leading part in exonerating Dr Ford.

It soon became apparent that the "new theology" espoused by Ford was prospering under a sympathetic administration. The editor of the Australasian Record and Australasian Signs of the Times, himself one of the BRI Committee, co-operated to the full by affording generous space in these magazines for the furthering of Fordian theology. It is not surprising then, that Conference presidents soon got the message and provided Avondale's ministerial graduates with cosy enclaves from which they were able to freely dispense their new-found bargains in "cheap grace", and salvation in sin! It was as if Adventism had suddenly burst forth from the restraining bonds placed around it by ignorant pioneers and a false prophetess.

The possibilities of church growth as a result of abolishing the restraints of obedience to God's law must have loomed largely in their vision of a popular and successful evangelical church. Love, not doctrine, would be their key to success from now on. But little did they realise that within some three years, their oracle would be fired and the downward plunge of homeland church growth would accelerate to the point of virtual stagnation.

It is not surprising then, that their new-found gospel of "love" was not large enough to encompass "stubborn" ministers who persisted in supporting the now-discredited historic Adventism.    In March 1977, a group of concerned brethren led by veteran evangelist J.W. Kent, succeeded in meeting with Division President Parmenter, Division and Union leaders, and Dr Ford.    We will let the Standish brothers describe the meeting:

> On this occasion, the Concerned Brethren were
> informed that this meeting would be the last
> time they could approach leadership as a
> group.  In the meeting, Dr Ford firmly main-
> tained his erroneous position, in spite of
> clear statements read to him from the Spirit
> of Prophecy. At the conclusion, the Division
> president and chairman, in ending the meet-
> ing, declared himself for Dr Ford, saying
> that never before had Dr Ford stood so high
> in his estimation as the present.  He also
> stated that he himself had problems in regard
> to our doctrine of the Sanctuary. Then turn-
> ing his head slightly in the direction of
> Pastor Burnside, he [Parmenter] warned in an
> intimidatory tone that if the attacks on Dr
> Ford continued, he would have them (the
> Concerned Brethren) dealt with.... In an
> earlier meeting the senior Concerned Brethren
> had been forcibly reminded by the Division
> president that Robert Brinsmead had been dis-
> fellowshiped, not for doctrinal deviation but
> for opposition to church authority. (Adven-
> tism Challenged p.280)

[Pastor A.P. Cooke, veteran evangelist, who was at this meeting confirmed the above report.]

With such arbitrary manifestations of "kingly power" and "popery" at Division level, it is not surprising that Conference presidents and others down the hierarchical line of power displayed similar conduct. Pastor O.K. Anderson, a veteran retiree living near Avondale, had already received a letter of censure from the then-president of the North N.S.W. Conference. It was written in response to Ford's complaints that Anderson had been counselling with some of his students at Avondale College. Part of the letter read:

I have carefully studied the position taken by the theology department of Avondale College. I see very little conflict and certainly no major conflict between the emphasis and that which I have stood for and preached for the last twenty years....

I would like to state in conclusion that I will make recommendation for your name to be included in the preaching plans for this conference, when I have evidence that you have dissociated yourself from the misrepresentation and subsequent attacks upon the Theology Department of Avondale College and upon Des Ford in particular. [Meaning he had removed Anderson from the preaching plan] You see, Brother Anderson, you have been too wise a counsellor and too long a servant in the cause of God, to go down in these latter years of your life, as one who supports unscholarly research and misrepresentation. I appeal to you to endeavour, with all your might to endeavour to understand what Dr Ford is endeavouring to say, without forming conclusions at every line and sentence.* (Dated 22nd Dec. 1976, signed by Athal Tolhurst.)

1.

Time and Ford's eventual dismissal have shown who stood in need of advice. At the time of writing, Pastor Anderson has not received an apology for this example of gross misuse of "kingly power" by incompetent leaders, nor has the ban on his preaching been officially lifted. Less than a year earlier, at the February BRI meetings, Tolhurst had cautiously expressed concern over Ford's teachings. Failure of Division leadership to act on his cue had apparently not been lost on Tolhurst. Was he now giving them a practical demonstration of his undoubted loyalty by backing Ford?

Other presidents soon followed suit. Within two years, the president of Greater Sydney Conference, Pastor K. Bullock had instructed the ministers of his conference by letter to deny Pastors J.W. Kent and G. Burnside the use of their pulpits. Once again, the reason behind the ban was to protect the jewel in the crown of Australian Adventism, Desmond Ford. He had been exposed in a pamphlet written by the two pastors for retailing Plymouth Brethren and Jesuitical inspired futuristic interpretation of the man of sin in his thesis for Manchester University. (For contents of letter dated 18th Dec. 1978, see Adventism Challenged, p. 316)

By this time, Ford was on loan to the theology department of Pacific Union College. No doubt it was with some pride that the Australasian administration had agreed to allow "Dr Seventh-day Adventist" to share his "advanced" doctrinal insights with less "enlightened" Adventists in North America.

But in the providence of God, it was not realised that this decision was soon to lead to a time of trouble such as the Australasian Division had never seen. It is now a matter of history that those entrusted with the preservation of the faith in North America took their ordination vows far more seriously than their counterparts in Australasia – or, as seen in hindsight, some at least wanted to appear to take their responsibilities seriously.

At the now-historic Glacier View meetings of August 1980, Ford's position, which he had been given six months to re-consider, was found to be doctrinally unacceptable. His main problem revolved around adventism's sanctuary message and consequently in the related and very important area of righteousness by faith. (See Ministry magazine, October, 1980 for official report) It will be remembered that in the above area of doctrine, Ford had been exonerated by the Australasian leadership in 1976.

Strangely, Ford's affection for the Roman Catholic invention of original sin and its corollary, a make-believe Saviour who did not inherit our human nature, did not appear to be an issue. Perhaps this is an indication that most of the Adventist ministry had been so dazzled by authors like L.E. Froom, that they failed to see vital connection between the heresy of the "unfallen nature" and righteousness by the kind of faith which does not require obedience.

What a shock it must have been to the administration of the Australasian Division when President Parmenter was instructed to pluck the jewel out of their "kingly" crown! It was now the credibility of the Australasian Division leadership which was at stake. And had not the president himself asserted to the concerned brethren that he also had problems in regard to our sanctuary doctrine?

President Parmenter now bent over backwards to save Ford and salvage what little credibility might be left for the leadership. He went so far as to publicly plead with Ford to compromise his considered beliefs by holding them **"in abeyance and not discussed unless at sometime in the future they might be found compatible with the positions and beliefs of the Seventh-day Adventist Church."** (Ministry Magazine Oct. 1980)

And so the Adventist world was treated to the spectacle of a Divison president pleading with a man to remain in the role of keeper of the faith, knowing full well that he did not believe in what God's messenger has identified as the foundation of the Adventist message.(Evangelism p.221) And while being supported by the sacred tithe, he was invited to deliberately refrain from preaching the three angels' messages in all their fullness and beauty! And then, horror of horrors, the president makes known his implied expectation that the time will come when the church's doctrinal positions may change sufficiently to allow Ford to preach the very heresies for which he had just been fired!*    2.

It would be encouraging to know that Ford rejected such a hypocritical invitation. But, this does not appear to be so. The Secretary of the Australasian Division, Pr R.W. Taylor circulated an undated leaflet explaining the circumstances of Ford's dismissal. It told how Ford had met with president Neal C Wilson and vice-president L.L. Bock and promised to refrain from speaking on doctrines unique to Adventism. That would, of course, include the sanctuary, investigative judgment and the Spirit of Prophecy. So it does appear, according to Taylor, that Ford accepted Parmenter's offer. But Taylor claims that Wilson and Bock said that it was improper for a minister of the SDA church to be silent on two such distinctive matters of doctrine.

Such a proper decision highlights the fundamental weakness that had become almost endemic to top Australasian leadership. They had simply lost sight of the church's mission to preach all three angels' messages! What a picture! Here is a division leader telling Ford to stay on and be silent, while world leaders tell Ford that it's no use being a Seventh-day Adventist minister unless he preaches the unique message entrusted to Adventism.*          3.

So it was, that the many loyal Adventists who had expressed their deep concerns over the inroads of heresy through the Administration's protection of Ford had been vindicated. Naturally, they could expect the issue to be settled once and for all and look forward to their church utilizing its energies and facilities fully in the proclamation of the "everlasting gospel". Pastor Athal Tolhurst, president of the North N.S.W. Conference apparently thought so. He called a meeting of regional churches to be held in the large Avondale College Auditorium. No doubt, encouraged by the top-level decision against Ford's theology, he recounted the events leading up to and at Glacier View, and enthusiastically proclaimed himself for the old time religion. But he was in for a shock! Not all his listeners agreed with him, for he was right on the home ground of Fordism.

Within a short time a meeting of the Australian Forum* was convened in the College. Two          4. theology lecturers who had attended the Glacier View meetings gave quite a different version of proceedings. They let it be known that Ford had many supporters at Glacier View and that the decision to fire Ford had been neither unanimous nor popular. These two men were delegated (obviously with Pastor Parmenter's permission) to travel around the Division spreading their disquieting story to the workers. In the process, much sympathy was generated for Ford.

It was soon perceived by many that Fordism was still alive and well in Australasia. God in His mercy had given the leadership a marvellous opportunity to admit their terrible mistake, to repent and turn the church around in the direction of historic Adventism. But pride and use of "kingly power", the hallmarks of papal-like government re-established in the General Conference in 1903, had now become the norm in the Australasian Division. Elder Figuhr's advice given in Melbourne back in the mid-fifties, regarding the selection of leaders, had long since become common practice. Harmony and unity, a political formulae for success, had become paramount. Therefore, no admission of errors of judgment or wrongful action, particularly against loyal watchmen, must ever reach the ears of the laity. All must appear to be well with the Seventh-day Adventist church!

*1.It should be noted that Tolhurst was not creating a precedent in acting on Ford's complaints. Pr. O.K. Anderson told the author that during the early seventies, President Rex Moe, while on the Avondale College Board, had telephoned him requesting that he refrain from disturbing Ford's students by refuting Ford's teaching.Later the Division president, Pr R.R. Frame, in 1975, had acted on complaints by Ford and issued instructions to the President of the South Australian Conference to prevent Pr. Anderson from preaching at the invitation of the Prospect Church Pastor. (Also reported in Adventism Challenged p.319) So it is apparent, that well before the BRI meetings of Feb. 1976, the Division leadership had decided not only to back Ford, but to use the office of "kingly power" to repress any who stood in the way of "Dr Seventh-day Adventist".

*2. In view of some subsequent publications of the SDA church written by Morris Venden, Helmut Ott's book, <u>Perfect in Christ</u> and the general acceptance of Fordian teaching on righteousness by faith in the South Pacific Division, Parmenter's expectation of "compatibility" must surely have been realized ere now.

*3. This fundamental weakness, denoting lack of true purpose, remains in the South Pacific Division to this day. Pr D.B.Hills, president of the Trans-Australia Union, in defending presidents against the charge that they knowingly employ Fordian ministers, makes this astounding admission:- "The leadership of the church that I am associated with are fully aware that there are people who don't teach error but also don't teach all the truths of the Word of God". (Letter to H.H. Meyers dated 1 Feb. 1989)

*4. Adventist Forums:
The Association of Adventist forums - a lay organisation whose purpose is "to encourage thoughtful persons of SDA orientation to examine and discuss freely ideas and issues relevant to the church in all its aspects and to its members as Christians in society". Publishes <u>Spectrum</u>, a journal of essays, book reviews, art and poetry. Organised 1967...framed its constitution after extensive consultation with G.C. officials, chaired by N.C. Wilson, then vice-president of Nth America. ..At the 1967 Annual Council, the Nth American Division Committee on Administration recognised the organisation stating, as reported in <u>R&H</u> Jan 11, 1968, that "we express sympathy with the stated aims and objectives of the proposed association" and "our desire to co-operate as far as possible in the development of any means which will serve to make this relationship more meaningful and mutually beneficial". (<u>SDA Encyclopedia</u> p.87)

"If any of you lack wisdom, let him ask of God, that giveth to all men liberally, and upbraideth not; and it shall be given him." Mercy and love and wisdom are to be found in God; but many who profess to know Him have turned from the One in whom our hope of eternal life is centred, and have educated themselves to depend upon their erring and fallible fellowmen. They are crippled spiritually when they do this; for no man is infallible, and his influence may be misleading. He who trusts in man not only leans upon a broken reed, and gives Satan an opportunity to introduce himself, but he hurts the one in whom the trust is placed; he becomes lifted up in his estimation of himself, and loses the sense of his dependence upon God. Just as soon as man is placed where God should be, he loses his purity, his vigor, his confidence in God's power. Moral confusion results, because his powers become unsanctified and perverted. He feels competent to judge his fellowmen, and he strives unlawfully to be a god over them.

E.G. White
Testimonies to Ministers, p. 376.

# CHAPTER 19

# CONFLICTING CLAIMS

The residents of Australia's largest city, Sydney, awoke to another work-a-day morning on May 2, 1983. But many Seventh-day Adventists were in for a second awakening, albeit a rude one, before the day was much older.

As they opened the pages of the Sydney Daily Telegraph newspaper, their eyes were transfixed by the bold headline **"SEVENTH-DAY CRISIS"**. Sure enough, the double page spread was all about troubles in their beloved church. The writer, Ken Anderson, described himself both as a writer for the Telegraph and as a "dissident Adventist minister" who expected to get the sack as a result of his revelations regarding the theological problems and unsavoury practices of the Seventh-day Adventist church.

"Did you know that the only people entitled to records of the legal Association and Trust Funds of the Seventh-day Adventist church are the top Administrators?" he asked.

Anderson claimed that his article was based on the results of an investigation "with both dissident scholars and ministers and established church leaders" and upon examination of books, documents, balance sheets and "other financial records not normally made available to the public and on an authoritative survey".

"The survey also shows that 67% of members have been influenced by Des Ford, the pastor who taught theology to hundreds of students at Avondale College, including Michael Chamberlain."

In defence, Secretary of the Division, Pr.Ron Taylor was reported as playing down the church's problems:

> About two or three years ago a number of members, not a majority by any means, were asking, "What's going on?" but not today. People are saying now, "We know where we stand so let's get on with it."

As for suggestions that the lay people of the church were victims of a bureaucratic hierarchy, the Division Communication Director, Pr. Russell Kranz also got into the act:

> The Adventist Church is possibly the most democratic in the world. Lay members have a representative form of government right to the very top.*      1.

Taylor then denied any flirtation of the church with Fordian doctrine:

> If Des Ford's beliefs were accepted they would be destructive to the church because he is hitting at areas of belief which the church holds to be fundamental.

(While Taylor's reasoning is perfectly correct, the reader will recall that the Division, through the Biblical Research Institute, had already accepted Ford's doctrinal stance on the grounds that he was in agreement with other Adventist writers and scholars. (See Chapter 17) This finding has never been rescinded officially.)

As if this public airing of Adventist "dirty washing" was not embarrassing enough, Adventists were again subjected to another double-page dose of "investigative" journalism the following day:

> Australian-born dissident church man, Dr. Des

Ford, says the Seventh-day Adventist Church faces a future in which it will be composed of those who don't care and those who don't think.
It needs to let lay people have a much bigger say in decision-making. The Bible teaches that there are no masters, that we are all brethren and every church member is on equal footing with any minister and every administrator.

The futility of equivocation should be apparent to the reader. In this case, the Administration has failed to please both Fordians and true Adventists alike. Truly, "no man can serve two masters".

Other aspects of the "investigative" report informed the public of the Davenport scandal and the supposed irregularities of Mrs E.G. White as a prophetess. Interestingly, no article of objection by the Division appeared in the Daily Telegraph over the next few days, nor does it appear that any "Letter of Objection" was written to its editor.

Obviously, such reporting was not inspired by those who had an abiding love for God's remnant church. The term "dissident" is correctly applied to such informers. But pride and "kingly power" were not to be unseated by such malicious exposure. The cloak would be drawn even tighter and the time would come when the administration of the Australasian Division would come to transfer the term "dissidents" from those who so confessed, to those who opposed the administration's devious ways.

It is not surprising then, that confidence in the Administration of the church slumped to an all-time low. This was reflected by an inordinate increase in apostasies which had brought church growth to a virtual standstill. By 1982, the annual increase for the two home Unions had slumped to less than four hundred while the statistical report for 1983 was entirely omitted from the Australasian Record. In 1984, the Trans Australia Union Conference actually sustained a membership loss of 166 souls! (When studying statistical reports of the South Pacific Division, it should be noted that by far the largest growth rate is in the Island Unions.)

*1. How different is Kranz's claim for Adventist Church government from that of the administration! It will be shown in Chapter 25, how the G.C. endeavoured to convince a U.S. District Court that the Adventist Church is governed by a hierarchy.

# CHAPTER 20

# DECEPTION OR
# WISHFUL THINKING?

It was into such confusion that Pr Walter R.L. Scragg entered when he assumed the presidency of the Australasian Division in 1984. Would he set about to remove the "dagger" from the bleeding heart of Adventism? Would he insist on the ministry and the church's educators upholding and teaching the three angels' messages in the manner of the pioneers who had so successfully proclaimed the everlasting gospel in all its fullness? Would he give the trumpet a 'certain sound' with a clarion call to 'come out of Babylon'? Would he encourage his flock to live sanctified lives in readiness for that great moment when their names must inevitably appear before the great Judge?

Apparently the president did not see things that way. It was not long before he was soothing the membership with joyful messages. The May 5, 1984 edition of the Record contained a message from the president titled, "Arms of Joy". After copious doses of the NEB's version of Biblical examples of joy, Pr Scragg was encouraged to dispense a little of his own:

> Joy comes from accepting the positive action of God, on your own behalf, another's behalf, on the church's behalf. The record accessions of our church in recent years, the perilous but successful stemming of the currents of false doctrine, the upsurge in interest in personal holiness, the fast fulfilling of the signs of our Lord's return, these create joy for God's action on behalf of his church.

If such a statement were all true, it would indeed be cause for great rejoicing. As we have already seen, church growth in the homelands was almost non-existent. If indeed, the homelands had shared in these record accessions (for they were virtually confined to Unions in the Mission field), this would only serve to highlight the extra-ordinary increase in apostasies. As for "the successful stemming of the currents of false doctrine", the president must have been almost alone in noticing it, unless of course, his perception of false doctrine differed from those who adhered to historic Adventism.

The author of this book wrote two letters to the president asking him to identify the "false doctrine" to which he referred. But to this day he has declined to identify even one! Many are still looking in bewilderment for evidences of the increased interest in "personal holiness", an attribute which rightly applies to personages of the Godhead but which has been misappropriated by the "Man of Sin".

Later in the same year, 1984, an article appeared in the Adventist Review (Oct 4) titled "Progress After Pain". It was a report on the Australasian Division compiled by Editor Dr Wm. Johnsson. He presented to the world a Division whose doctrinal controversy was apparently a thing of the past. But President Scragg was quick to realise that here, for the first time, was a specific announcement to the world of Adventism, of past serious doctrinal problems with all its attendant pain. He quickly moved to minimise the admission by placing an explanatory letter in the Review, Nov. 8, 1984:

> In understanding the situation [as described by Johnsson], readers should be aware that the 'internal wrangling', 'bitter spirit' and

'brother arguing against brother' were limited to a relatively small number of people in a few restricted areas.

Possibly, the most generous assessment of such a statement is to attribute it to the ignorance of one who had not been present in the Australasian Division during those years of "pain". But the pain was to continue. Loyal Adventists had to sit in their pews and endure sermons that not only lacked the certainties of the judgment-hour message, but in many cases, listen to outright attacks on our distinctive doctrines and on the pioneers who propounded them.

The obvious lack of doctrinal and prophetic emphasis in our pulpits lent credibility to a widely-held belief that such practice conformed to leadership's policy. Is it a mere coincidence that some of our leaders attended Heppenstall's Avondale lectures in 1957/58? (See Chapter 15, p.89) It is no wonder then, that groups of sincere Adventists banded together in order to hear the straight message. Soon, message-hungry members were flocking to hear the full gospel preached in meetings described by some administrators as "unauthorised". Instead of recognising the symptoms of spiritual starvation and applying the obvious remedy, President Scragg led his officers in opposing those who "illegally" dispensed the words of life, as witness the following example:

For many years, Australian brothers Colin and Russell Standish have been employed in educational and medical work respectively, by Seventh-day Adventist organisations abroad. Periodically, while at home on furloughs, they have been giving the trumpet a certain sound while conducting meetings at the invitation of discerning Adventist groups. Usually, they were denied the use of church facilities and venues for such meetings. While these meetings brought much spiritual joy and encouragement to many members, they also brought much unhappiness to some presidents who felt that they had been endowed with the divine right of determination as to whom their members may listen.

Following complaints by the then-president of North NSW, A.D.C. Currie and Trans-Tasman Union Conference President Athal Tolhurst, concerning "unauthorised" meetings by Dr Colin Standish, Division President Walter Scragg decided to act. He forwarded a copy of Currie's letter of complaint (with its false accusations – see Anchor Nov. 1985 "No fruit For The Master") to the President of the North American Division, C.E. Bradford. For good measure, he included a covering letter of his own which said in part:-

I regret to have to write to you regarding the activities of one of our Australian brethren who is working in North America. However we feel that you should know that the activities of Colin Standish in our Division are far from constructive. You can see the nature and extent of the problem and the way it troubles the church in Australasia. I believe it would be well if the administrative body which governs the Hartland Institute should be advised of the activities of Dr Standish in the hope that they might be able to give him counsel on how to conduct himself while on furlough.

There is a problem with individuals such as Colin Standish who are not under direct Conference direction but relate rather to the Association of Self-Supporting Industries. I recognise that it is a difficult and complex issue but we would like as much assistance as you are able to give to endeavour to control some of his activities. (Wahroonga, March 19, 1985)

Thankfully, such ill advice was not accepted, for no attempt was made to apply the rod of "kingly power". Dr Standish continues in his position as president of Hartland Institute and continues to exercise his God-given commission to preach the gospel according to the light conferred upon His remnant church.

But this striking rebuff has not deterred President Scragg in his quest for authoritarian control over his vast section of popedom.* He has consistently evidenced a zealous watch over itinerant speakers that would be highly laudable were it applied to those who are bringing Babylonian doctrines into our church. But, as an example, we will continue with the South Pacific Division's apparent pre-occupation with disciplining Dr Standish.

The Hartland Institute, a self-supporting Adventist ministry in Virginia, USA, has sponsored many Firm Foundation conferences throughout North America, Europe and Australasia. Dr Colin Standish is the president of Hartland. Some sixteen months prior to coming to Australia, Dr Standish approached the administration of the South Pacific Division for their support. But the Division President let Dr Standish know that the Firm Foundation meetings were not needed, nor were they wanted. This is quite understandable in the light of the president's false claim of "the successful stemming of the currents of false doctrine" (Record May 5, 1984, "Arms of Joy" article).

The Firm Foundation meetings went ahead,

nevertheless, during the summer of 1986/87. One
president desperately attempted to discredit the
campaign as a means by which local conference
finances could be depleted.  An Anchor reporter
said:

> In the West Australian conference, each min-
> ister and elder was circulated with a letter
> falsely stating that the Firm Foundation con-
> ferences took large sums of money from Europe
> for Hartland Institute. [Yet, four months
> earlier, Dr Colin Standish had personally
> answered this charge to the South Pacific
> Division President.]
> The specific charge was that 800,000 guilders
> (about $500,000) was taken from Holland in
> donation...The facts are that about $400.00
> worth of books were sold and this was the
> only money received and taken out.(Anchor No.
> 10, p.2)

Such a flagrant example of irresponsible
reporting is probably indicative of the despera-
tion of a Division that has lost its vision and
its way. But it seems that by early 1989, President Scragg was able at last to savour the
satisfaction of being able to announce a successful result to his persistent efforts.
The occasion was a workers' retreat at
Yarrahapini, NSW, where he announced that Colin
Standish's ministerial credentials had been
revoked.  The news soon spread throughout the
homeland Unions with the rapidity of a scandal.
Had the report been based on fact, and had it
been the result of a misdemeanour, one wonders
just how people whose priority should be the
preaching of the three angels' messages, would
find the time and inclination to damage the
reputation of the ministry by spreading such

appalling news!

But once again, the report was nothing more than a rumour spawned by the wishful thinking of some whose priorities undoubtedly must be suspect. Several letters of protest have since been written by members of the Standish family to Division, Union and Conference leadership, some of which have been circulated extensively amongst leadership.

As many of the concerns expressed therein are indicative of the general situation now prevailing in the South Pacific Division, some have been reprinted in full or in part in the Appendix. Read them while keeping in mind the type of organization described by Mrs White as a "kingly power" and by A.T. Jones variously as a "Czarist" oligarchy and a "papal" hierarchy.

*1.According to Pr George Burnside, who attended the New Orleans General Conference, President N.C. Wilson several times referred to his Division Presidents as 'Cardinals' (Conversation between Burnside and author 1988. This is corroborated by Dr R.R. Standish in a conversation with the author, 1989)

The souls who love God, who believe in Christ, and who eagerly grasp every ray of light, will see light, and rejoice in the truth. They will communicate the light. They will grow in holiness. Those who receive the Holy Spirit will feel the chilling atmosphere that surrounds the souls of others by whom these great and solemn realities are unappreciated and spoken against. They feel that they are in the council of the ungodly, of men who stand in the way of sinners, and sit in the set of the scornful...

Yet many have listened to the truth spoken in demonstration of the Spirit, and they have not only refused to accept the message, but they have hated the light. These men are parties to the ruin of souls. They have interposed themselves between the heaven—sent light and the people. They have trampled upon the word of God and are doing despite to His Holy Spirit.

E.G. White
Testimonies to Ministers, p.90,91.

# CHAPTER 21

# HIERARCHY IN ACTION

---

In keeping with the Adventists' desperate attempts to convince a United States District Court that the government of the S.D.A. church is papal in structure (which will be described in Chapter 25), we may expect to find an authoritarian attitude extending right down the hierarchical chain of command – through Division presidents, Union presidents, Conference presidents and thence through conference workers and church pastors. Let us briefly look at the chain of command in the South Pacific Division, not only to see if it is authoritarian in nature, but also to find out its true objective. Does it advance the cause espoused by the Adventist pioneers or does it aid the slide towards Rome?

We have noted at some length, Division President Scragg's attitude to Dr Colin Standish's speaking at "unauthorised" meetings – he was unappreciative. Yet Colin's audiences were very enthusiastic. Which simply adds up to the fact that they were listening to messages which they seldom hear.

Similarly, other visiting and local preachers find their "unauthorised" meetings in considerable demand. One such preacher is veteran retired evangelist, Pastor Austin P. Cooke. In this connection, let us now look at the Union presidents and discover their administrative attitudes. Do they render allegiance to God and the divine commission given to the remnant church or do they bow to the wishes of man?

We have two Union Conferences in the homelands of the South Pacific Division – the Trans

Tasman Union with headquarters in Sydney and the Trans Australia Conference, controlled from Melbourne. Both the Union Presidents, Pr Harold Harker and Pr Desmond Hills respectively, know what historic Adventism is all about and to the best of the author's knowledge, are quite capable of preaching it. Indeed, both have publicly stated in the hearing of the author, their unswerving allegiance to preaching the three angels' messages .*

Seventh-day Adventist retired ministers receive their honorary credentials through the Union in which they reside. It is the president's duty to know about the suitability of those to whom his committee issues credentials. There are certain guidelines laid down in the church manual regarding church discipline. From page 158 of the Church Manual we read:

> No individual member or group of members should start a movement or form an organization or seek to encourage a following for the attainment of any objective, or the teaching of any doctrine or message not in harmony with the fundamental religious objectives and teachings of the Seventh-day Adventist Church.

Now, surely one would not be presumptuous in regarding Dr Desmond Ford's Good News Australia magazine as the official organ of an organization that falls within this category, for Ford is still (early 1989) a member of the S.D.A. church.*

We have already noted at some length (Chapter 14) where a retired minister, Pr V. Heise, credentialed in the T.T.U.C., openly supported Ford's organization by contributing an article to Good News Australia (Sep. 1988) Surely any member, especially a minister, who so boldly identifies with the ideals of Ford's organization cannot, according to the Manual, be considered a loyal church member, let alone hold ministerial credentials issued by the SDA church!

On the 23rd February 1989, the author wrote to the President of the Trans Tasman Union Conference expressing concern. Enclosed was a copy of Heise's article. In reply, Pr Harker attempted to dodge the main issue - that of public support for Ford - with the following diversionary remarks:

> There was nothing in the article that could be seen "as cause for disciplinary action..." I also do not see Pr Vern Heise, who is retired, forming a new organization or trying to get a following. (Letter March 16, 1989)

However, to his credit, he did eventually get around to addressing the real concern of the author by noting before closing that:

> "...It does tell where sympathies lie and this should be noted." (Ibid)

During the latter part of May 1989, the T.T.U.C. Executive met in session and Pr Heise's credentials were left intact. But those of veteran, Pr Austin Cooke, who publicly upholds historic Adventism and denounces error, were revoked! (Letter from Harker to Cooke, 23rd May, 1989)

Meanwhile, in the Trans Australia Union Conference, a lay member of the S.D.A. church had been recently admitted into church employment as a high school teacher. He also, had publicly supported Ford by writing articles appearing in <u>Good News Australia</u>. On the 26th Jan.

1989 the author wrote to T.A.U.C. president, Pr
D. Hills expressing general concern:
> that so many of our Administrators knowingly
> employ men whose interpretation of truth
> coincides with Des Ford's Reformationist
> concept of Righteousness by Faith and other
> views aberrant to Seventh-day Adventism. Need
> I remind you of the great influence our
> teachers have upon our youth and the signifi-
> cance of placing Fordian teachers in our
> church schools?

In reply (1st Feb. 1989) Pr Hills stated:
> It is not true that 'many of our administra-
> tors knowingly employ men whose interpre-
> tations of the truth coincides with Des
> Ford's' etc.

Then followed an astounding admission:
> **The leadership of the church that I am assoc-
> iated with are fully aware that there are
> people who don't preach error but also don't
> preach all of the Word of God.**

He then defended the teacher on the grounds
that his president didn't "know of this church
member teaching views held by Des Ford or
withholding truths upheld by the Seventh-day
Adventist Church". Apparently these remarks were
primarily based on the fact that the teacher in
question had taught Sabbath School classes and
came "with positive recommendations as a loyal
Seventh-day Adventist".

In this case, the president of the T.A.U.C.
entirely ignored the point of concern – that the
teacher was sufficiently supportive of Ford to
declare his position publicly – so he ignored
it! The author replied, 17th Feb. 1989, pointing

out that:

> You have ducked the question of employing
> Fordian sympathisers. ...May I point out to
> you that you are being given the opportunity
> to give credibility to your numerous affirma-
> tions (of loyalty to Adventists' perception
> of truth.)

In reply, President Hills sought to minimise
the impact of his admission by stating that:

> You need to note that the statement was made
> with reference to 'people' and you are not
> correct in presuming that that's specifically
> stated 'church employees'.

But, the careful reader will note that the
concern expressed in the correspondence has been
only about people employed by the church.

By now, it must be evident that in a hierarchical system of administration, even though
an administrator may be inclined to act to uphold the standards required for the preservation
of Adventist beliefs and ideals, it is most
unlikely that subordinates will act against the
direction of their superiors.  If they were so
in the habit, it is not likely they would have
attained their position on the ladder of hierarchy.  But the end result is that both the two
homeland Unions are administratively tolerant of
Fordian supporters – a fact which contrasts with
their attitude shown towards some ministers who
are openly loyal to historic Adventism.

We now come down the ladder of hierarchy to
conference level. In the North New South Wales
Conference, of which Pr Rex Moe is president,
some curious methods have been used in
"advancing" God's work. A recent spate of
disfellowshipments and resignations indicate a

surfacing of an undercurrent of disenchantment with what is seen as evidence of "kingly", "papal-like" power.

Pr Moe took upon himself the task of shutting down the Anchor magazine.* During a special business meeting of the Avondale Memorial Church, 27th Sept. 1987, he claimed that the Anchor's charges that the Australasian Division had accepted apostasy when they had exonerated Ford at the Biblical Research Institute's meetings back in 1976 were untrue, mainly on the grounds that at that time Ford had not declared his apostate position.

Yet the editor of Anchor was able to produce two witnesses (who were in attendance at the B.R.I. meetings) to say that President Rex Moe had vigorously defended Ford, especially in connection with Ford's claim that the earth's age was considerably more than 6,000 years. Moe hotly objected to this testimony, saying that he had always been comfortable with Sis. White's position – that the earth is around 6,000 years old.

But the editor had come into possession of a curious set of papers which President Moe, through his committee, had arranged to circulate quietly among his workers. These papers were written and prepared by one of his ministers, Pr S.R. Goldstone, who had taken the liberty of entitling them "The Seventh-day Adventist Church Believes..." (He had beaten the G.C. Ministerial Association to the punch with their book Seventh-day Adventists Believe...)

Quite a deal of Resource material accompanied Goldstone's comments on each of the fundamentals. Each section of the fundamentals was preceded with a full page on which appeared a large cautionary notice written in Goldstone's handwriting:

**Resource Material only. Please use with discretion.**

But preceding a section containing some forty of Mrs White's quotations bearing on the earth's age, appeared an extra injunction:

**Note that the Bible nowhere makes statements regarding the age of the earth. It is adamant that God was the Creator. Where the Bible is silent we ought to be silent.\*** 4.

The editor then produced this evidence before the assembled business meeting, showing that some twelve years on from Ford's BRI meetings, we have a president who denies supporting Ford, yet is presently assisting in the distribution of Fordian material which casts doubts not only on the denomination's understanding of the age of the earth, but also by implication, on the Spirit of Prophecy!

The fact that this sort of material is being circulated to the ministry with a caution as to how it is used, raises grave implications, for obviously it is not intended for the eyes of the laity. But other ideas are quietly injected into the minds of the ministry. In the section dealing with fundamental No 23, p.10, relating to our distinctive beliefs on the investigative judgment, Goldstone says:

**The conclusion reached by the consensus of scholars within the Seventh-day Adventist Church is that the Book of Hebrews neither confirms nor denies our belief in the Investigative Judgment.**

In fairness to Goldstone, we here record that he claims to believe in an investigative judgment but he gets his belief from an overall view of the Bible - not just Hebrews. But even this affirmation gets a watering down:

> I believe the primary purpose of the investi-gative judgment is to vindicate God's name before His intelligent creatures. God is on trial more than men. (p.13)

But his view is strangely at variance with that of the pioneers who regarded the warnings of a personal judgment as a message to be urgently proclaimed.

It is no wonder that the ministry is cautioned over and over again to be discreet in their use of such information!

The next stage in the attempt to silence the Anchor took place just five months later - on 27th Feb. 1988. This time a Special Business meeting of the Avondale Memorial Church was called to consider disciplining the editor, H.H. Meyers, for continuing to publish Anchor. By church standards, this was an illegal meeting for it contravened the clear rules of the church manual:

> No church officer should advise, no committee should recommend, nor should any church vote, that the name of a wrongdoer shall be removed from the church books, until the instruction given by Christ has been faithfully followed. (Church Manual p.155)

Christ's instructions, as mentioned in the manual are to be found in Matt. 18. Surely these would require that the church Pastor with a church elder would have visited the editor! But it seems that silencing those who "sigh and cry" has such priority that Christ's instructions don't apply, for neither the church pastor nor

the president nor anyone delegated by the church
came to discuss the matter with editor Meyers.*    5.
No one even bothered to ascertain whether or not
the time  for the disciplinary  meeting was con-
venient to the "erring one".

However, the President did show his interest
by attending the meeting.  He sat there and by
his silence condoned the efforts to discredit
the editor and then watched a motion instigated
to have the editor disfellowshipped.  But he was
in for a surprise!  He was forced to witness the
scheming and conspiring of some eighteen months
come undone.  By secret ballot, the motion was
lost - 101 votes to 54!

Had church Pastor J. Beamish followed the
injunction of Christ and had dialogue with the
editor, he could have learned that he had been
negotiating for several months  with new editors
who were about to take over.  In the event, the
meeting was a big fuss over nothing, for by this
time, Meyers was no longer the editor! One cannot escape the conclusion that if similar plan-
ning and energy were directed towards spreading
the third angel's message, there would be no
need for journals like the Anchor.

Pastor Ross Goldstone has since been appointed pastor of the Avondale Memorial Church.
Pastor Austin Cooke has had his membership there
during the previous eight years of his retirement.  Never once in all these years has he been
invited to preach in divine service or take a
Sabbath School lesson.  It is no wonder then,
that he commenced fellowshipping in another
church, at nearby Boolaroo.  There he has been
able to participate by teaching Sabbath School
lessons.

In November 1988, he applied to have his
membership transferred to Boolaroo church.  But,

by the 17th April 1989, at the time of an Avondale Memorial Church business meeting, his transfer had still not been put to the Church for vote. Pastor Cooke requested at this meeting that in view of the inordinate delay, his transfer be put to the vote and settled at that very meeting.

Pr Goldstone, who chaired the meeting, flatly refused. After difficult attempts to question him, it appeared that he was awaiting advice from the Trans Tasman Union Conference.

This unusual procedure seems to denote a lack of confidence in a credentialing system that has shown confidence in Pr Cooke throughout his outstandingly successful evangelistic career. Is this part of a popish pattern in the South Pacific Division to suppress the teaching of established truth? In Pastor Cooke's case, his standing as a church member is under question, simply because he has offended an authoritarian system by moving around the Division giving truth-starved church members the historic Adventist message and denouncing apostasy. In years gone by, such commitment would be lauded by conference presidents. Why not now?

Which brings us to another important sphere of Division influence - Avondale College, and in particular, its theology department. This is the college which was brought into being under the direct guidance of God through Mrs E.G. White. Our pioneers denied themselves in order to have a "School for Christian Workers". Later it became known as the "Australasian Missionary College" and as such it has been eminently successful. But now it is known as Avondale College, a "college of higher learning". The management still claim to run a "blue-print" college.

This is where young church members train to

be Seventh-day Adventist ministers, but having studied Babylonian theology, not all of them know what Seventh-day Adventism is supposed to be about. One recent graduate had to ask the meaning of the term "three angels' messages"!

The theology department is very sensitive to criticism. Around the end of 1988, a video tape was produced by a lecturer in evangelism at Avondale College, Pastor Graeme Bradford. It was directed against the preaching of a veteran retired minister, who, while exposing apostate Adventism had brought the college into it. This tape has been quietly circulated around the conferences and played to selected audiences. Although Bradford frequently addresses the veteran by name, he had not bothered to advise him of the tape's existence, let alone afford him the courtesy of seeing it!

Discerning viewers of this video will be grateful for the fact that we now have an unequivocal admission from the theology department that they are in the track of Calvinistic-evangelical theology. Bradford follows Froom's ubtle approach in promoting "new theology", raises doubts on the competency of the pioneers by showing that new light demanded that they forsake Arianism; and from this attempts to have Mrs E.G. White infer that new light will continue to be revealed, (even on accepted truth).

Part of this "new light" appears to be old light revealed by the Roman Catholic church. Bradford comes down heavily for Augustine's invention of original sin, claiming that we are all born sinners except Christ who, because He didn't sin must have entered this world with a different nature from ours. But, quite unfairly, he fails to give credit to Augustine for his inventive genius which runs contrary to scripture (1 John 3:4) and claims that he gets this doctrine (of anti-christ, 1 John 4:3) from the Bible.

However can Bradford make the Bible contradict itself? It's quite simple! Rome has already provided him with her Roman corruptions of scripture and, in keeping with those who promote apostate Adventism, he turns to Rome for help. He reads from the Psalms, according to the NIV:

> Surely I have been a sinner from birth, sinful from the time my mother conceived me. (Psalms 51:5 NIV)

Says Bradford:

> That's the Word of God — sinner from birth.

But those who believe that "all scripture is given by inspiration of God" will know that God cannot contradict Himself. He says: "For sin is the transgression of the law" (1 John 3:4) And God's Messenger tells us that this is the only definition of sin in the Bible. (G C p.493) But God tells us in His Holy Word just what David really did say:

> Behold I was shapen in iniquity; and in sin did my mother conceive me. (Psa 51:5 KJV)

Bradford tries to tell his viewers that the KJV has the same meaning as given in the NIV. Then why did he cite the NIV? The reason is obvious — it doesn't. Bradford here shows that he does not believe the SDA Bible Commentary on this text. It says:

> David recognizes that children inherit natures with propensities to evil. (Vol 3, p.755)

Isn't that why God chose Mary to be Christ's

mother - so that Jesus would inherit a similar nature to that with which you and I started life?

The owner of the NIV copyright is the New York International Bible Society. Their Preface claims that their Bible is "a completely new translation ...made by over 100 scholars" and that it is "trans-denominational" i.e. suitable for a variety of denominations because it reflects the philosophy of the Christian Reformed Church and the National Association of Evangelicals. So it is an ecumenical Bible!

As with the KJV, the translators appear to rely on the Masoretic Text, but we are advised that there are "variant readings" not necessarily specified by footnotes. As the translators of the KJV also claim to rely on the Masoretic Text, then it seems that the NIV translators went elsewhere to translate Ps 51:5. Was it the Septuagint? No. The LXX agrees with the Masoretic from which the KJV derives:

> For, behold I was conceived in iniquities, and in sins did my mother conceive me. (The Septuagint Greek and English. Bagster)

We must search the NIV Preface again for clues. Here we are told that readings from the Juxta Hebraica of Jerome were occasionally used in the Psalms "where accepted principles of textual criticism showed that one or more of these textual witnesses appeared to provide the correct reading".

Well, that really gives us something to think about, doesn't it? We're told that the translators are associated with the Christian Reformed Church and the National Association of Evangelicals. If a reading seemed doubtful to their religious beliefs they simply searched for a "textual witness that appeared to provide a correct reading"; in this case, a reading that would uphold Augustine's invention of Original Sin.

But even Jerome, a friend and admirer of Augustine, was not able to translate Ps 51:5 so as to entirely support his friend's invention of original sin as translated in the NIV. A literal translation of his Latin Juxta Hebraica would read something like this:-

Behold, I was born in a condition of blame and in sin my mother conceived me.

(Recently, the author was browsing through a religious book shop in the Philippines. All the Bibles on display were R.C. publications with the exception of one other - the NIV!)

In his video, Bradford frequently identifies with the theology of most of the ministry in Australasia, which is not surprising. They too, have received ministerial training that is tainted, if not impregnated with Fordism. But Bradford's video reveals another identifying characteristic of a forlorn cause. He conducts an interview with a retired history professor who sets about to discredit our retired evangelist over a minor historical mistake which he is alleged to have made during a lecture some thirty years back - yes, thirty years ago!

As if that were not puerile enough, this frustrated professor then resorts to a vitriolic attack on God's veteran. He described what he perceived to be one of the evangelist's idiosyncrasies:

And so he feels free to make what amounts to be defamatory statements ...about people and institutions and does it with an inane neurotic laugh that you would expect to get from a fire-bug or a saboteur.

Is this an insight into the kind of "love" that is promoted by a theology that advocates more love and less doctrine?

How deplorable to realise that those who have been entrusted with the training of Seventh-day Adventist ministers have misdirected their time and talents in such destructive pursuits. But even more devastating is the realisation that there are presidents and/or other workers around the conferences who encourage such un-Christian and un-Adventist-like ventures by disseminating such a destructive video.

On the 4th June, 1989, during a meeting held to "enlighten" elders of the South Queensland conference at Kallangur, Pastor Bradford advertised this series of video tapes, assuring the elders that they had approval of South Pacific Division leadership. Conference president, David Lawson enthusiastically offered to help in the distribution. Then in the July edition of his Conference paper, Focus, Lawson took the opportunity to get Bradford's message to all of his constituents:

> If you did not hear Pastor Bradford at the Elders' Meeting, let me suggest you obtain a set of videos produced by Avondale College featuring Pr. Bradford ... etc.

Truly the experiences of the pioneers could well be emulated by our leaders today! God's Messenger says:

> We are to be established in the faith, in the light of the truth given us in our early experience... We would search the scriptures with much prayer, and the Holy Spirit would bring the truth to our minds... The power of God would come upon me, and I was enabled clearly to define what is truth and what is

error.
As the points of our faith were thus established, our feet were placed on a solid foundation. We accepted the truth point by point
under the demonstration of the Holy Spirit. I
would be taken off in vision, and explanations would be given me..."(Gospel Workers
pp.302) It is the enemy that leads minds off
on side-tracks (such as the Bradford video
tape). He is pleased when those who know the
truth become engrossed in collecting scriptures to pile around erroneous theories,
which have no foundation in truth. The scriptures thus used are mis-applied; they were
not given to substantiate error, but to
strengthen truth. (Ibid. p.303)

*1.Special Business meeting called in attempt to silence
Anchor magazine, Avondale Memorial Church (27th Sept.
1987)
*2.The fact that Dr Ford is allowed to remain a member of
the S.D.A. Church while contravening conditions of
membership laid down in the Church Manual, is another
issue to which President Neal Clayton Wilson apparently
turns a blind eye.
*3.A letter to the editor of Anchor magazine appeared in
"Anchor Lines" (Feb 1987 edition: "A friend of mine from
Glen Innes (North N.S.W.) claims that the President told
church members there, that "they" were going to deal with
the Editor and shut the Anchor up."
Further light on the wishful intentions of the administration is revealed in a South Queensland church bulletin
dated August 15, 1987.
    "Action was taken by the church where he [the Editor]
holds membership, to apply church discipline if he
continues to publish Anchor."
    In the event, such action was not initiated until Feb
27, 1988 over six months after the 'event' was announced!

A motion to disfellowship Meyers failed by 101:54! (See Anchor No 19, p.13 for report).

The Anchor magazine was brought into being in April 1985 to uphold historic Adventism and expose error. Its first editor was H.H. Meyers, an Adventist layman with membership at the Avondale Memorial church. It is presently being edited jointly by Ron and Ula Cable, and its continued success indicates the real need which it and other similar magazines fulfil. Back numbers and current copies may be obtained from:

The Editors, Anchor magazine

P.O.Box 19, KALBAR Queensland 4309 AUSTRALIA

*4 If the Bible nowhere makes statements on the age of the earth, then, by the same method of reasoning, it nowhere mentions the year 1844 as the start of the Investigative Judgment! There is no end to the possibilities of such specious reasoning.

*5.Another example of reckless dissemination of false information concerns President Scragg's correspondence concerning the Editor of Anchor.

In responding to a letter from a church member expressing surprise that Meyers had never been visited by the church pastor, Scragg said, "I know that the Conference president and church pastors have visited him more than once..." (Letter 13 Jan. 1988) But in reply to persistent correspondence, Scragg had to admit his error: "You are right; there have been no recent pastoral visits to Hilton Meyers". (Letter 21, April 1988) In fact, there had never been any pastoral visits to Meyers.

Unless the church, which is now being leavened with her own backsliding, shall repent and be converted, she will eat of the fruit of her own doing, until she shall abhor herself. When she resists the evil and chooses the good, when she seeks God with all humility and reaches her high calling in Christ, standing on the platform of eternal truth and by faith laying hold upon the attainments prepared for her, she will be healed. She will appear in her God-given simplicity and purity, separate from earthly entanglements, showing that the truth has made her free indeed. Then her members will indeed be the chosen of God, His representatives.

The time has come for a thorough reformation to take place. When this reformation begins, the spirit of prayer will actuate every believer and will banish from the church the spirit of discord and strife. Those who have not been living in Christian fellowship will draw close to one another....

E.G. White
Testimonies, Volume 8, p.250, 251.

# Chapter 22

# THIS WAY TO ROME

---

When we read in Adventist literature the oft-repeated term "apostate Protestantism" we understand that the author is talking about Protestant churches that are backsliding to Rome. When the Seventh-day Adventist Church accepts the teachings of apostate Protestantism and imitates the ways of Rome, it is logical to refer to that condition as apostate Adventism, for the very term "apostasy" denotes a turning back or backsliding from a position once espoused.

God's Messenger had no illusions as to the direction in which a backsliding church is headed:

> **It is a backsliding church that lessens the distance between itself and the Papacy.** (<u>Signs of the Times</u> Feb. 19, 1894)

We have seen how in 1903 the church deliberately defied God's will by returning to a type of bureaucratic government described by Mrs White as a "kingly power" and by A.T. Jones as "a government more like that of the papacy than any of the Protestant churches".(See Chapter 13)

We have also seen how the doctrinal changes brought into the Seventh-day Adventist church under the cloak of historic Adventism, have brought us into favour with popular evangelicalism. Let us now briefly examine the veracity of our Messenger's claim that such changes lead towards the papacy, by examining the two prongs of the dagger - namely the unfallen nature and the judgment in relation to a completed atonement.

## 1. God sending His own son in the likeness of sinful flesh (Rom. 8:3)

The Romanists have been trying to get the human nature of Christ as far away from our humanity as possible, and hence have taught the immaculate conception of Mary. (Bishop Simpson in his 'Yale Lectures on Preaching' Quoted in Bible Echo Dec 1897)

By the dogma of the immaculate conception of the Virgin Mary, Rome teaches that the mother of Jesus was preserved from the stain of 'original sin', and that she had sinless flesh. Consequently she was separated from the rest of humanity. As a result of the separating of Jesus from sinful flesh, the Roman priesthood has been instituted in order that there may be someone to mediate between Christ and the sinner. (Sabbath School Quarterly, second quarter 1913, p.25)

Ancient Babylon affirmed that the gods (or God) dwelt not in the flesh. By the dogma of the immaculate conception of the Virgin Mary (that is that she herself was born without a taint of original sin) modern Babylon teaches that God, in the person of His Son, did not take the same flesh with us; that is, sinful flesh. (Bible Readings for the Home Circle, 1915, p.236)

The Scripture plainly teaches that Jesus, when born of a woman, assumed sinful flesh (Heb.2:14; Rom. 8:3) and thus became united with man in his fallen condition. This doctrine of the immaculate conception of the Virgin Mary separates Jesus from the human family in its present state, by giving Him "perfect human nature" free from the stain of original sin, and thus prepares the way for the introduction of the human mediation which is one of the prominent features of the Roman Catholic system. The very essence of Christianity being the experience, "Christ in you, the hope of glory" it thus appears that the dogma of the immaculate conception of the Virgin Mary strikes at the very heart of Christianity. (Note by Editors, Source Book for Bible Students, p.220 R & H, 1919; deleted from 1922 edition)

In spite of such striking statements, all of which appear in official publications of the SDA church, the books Questions On Doctrine and Movement of Destiny uphold the Roman Catholic heresy which is dependant on the dogma of the immaculate conception.Both teach that Christ did not inherit a sinful human nature. Examples:
Took Sinless Human Nature (QOD p.650)
Took Sinless Nature of Adam Before Fall (MOD p.497)

2. **For God shall bring every work into judgment, with every secret thing, whether it be good or whether it be evil. (Ecclesiastes 12:14)**

**For there is one God and one mediator between God and men, the man Christ Jesus.(1Tim. 2:5)**

When a Seventh-day Adventist publication states "'Complete' Atonement Made on Cross" (MOD p.501) and "The atonement, or reconciliation was completed on cross as pre-shadowed by the sacrifices, and the penitent believer can trust in this finished work of our Lord" (Seventh-day Adventists Believe... p.315) the church's belief

in an atoning role of Christ in heaven as High
Priest and mediator is logically brought into
ridicule. In commenting on Adventism's changed
position, Barnhouse described our belief in the
Investigative Judgment as **"stale, flat and
unprofitable"** (Eternity, Sept. 1956)

But, as seen earlier in this chapter, the
Roman Catholic Church seeks to abort Christ's
role as heavenly High Priest by insinuating its
own mediators between God and man.   Satan is
determined one way or another to rob Jesus
Christ of His mediatorial role for which He
alone is qualified.

> Forasmuch then as the children are partakers
> of flesh and blood, he also himself likewise
> took part of the same; that through death he
> might destroy him that had the power of
> death, that is, the devil;
> And deliver them who through fear of death
> were all their lifetime subject to bondage.
> For verily he took not on him the nature of
> angels; but he took on him the seed of
> Abraham.
> Wherefore in all things it behoved him to be
> made like unto his brethren, that he might be
> a merciful and faithful high priest in things
> pertaining to God, to make reconciliation for
> the sins of the people.
> For in that he himself hath suffered being
> tempted, he is able to succour them that are
> tempted. (Heb. 2:14-18)

Whether Christ's work of Salvation is cut off
at the cross with a "completed act of atonement"
or whether His work is circumscribed by the
confines of a papal wafer in a virtual state of
perpetual crucifixion, is of little consequence
to the Archdeceiver. Either way, there is no

need for an investigative judgment – which is described by our prophet as Christ's final act of atonement.

By either means, man is not constrained to seek an intimate union with our Saviour by following "Jesus by faith into the heavenly sanctuary" (Early Writings p.255) Instead, he can delude himself that he need not obey God, for he is already saved at the cross, or by the incantations of a mystical human mediator:

> The holy eucharist is the sublime source of this intimate union with Jesus Christ during man's earthly pilgrimage, for in receiving holy communion, the Christian soul may truly exclaim: "And I live, now not I, but Christ liveth in me" Gal. 2:20. (The Catholic Church the True Church of the Bible" pp. 132,133, quoted in Source Book for Bible Students, 1919 p.297; 1922 edition p. 319)

But in recent years, Adventists have come up with an ingenious Clayton-like* device consist-  1. ing of a judgment which you have when you're not being judged! The term "Investigative Judgment" is far too descriptive for some, so they prefer to call it the "Pre-Advent Judgment".

They tell us that its primary purpose is to give the universe an opportunity to judge God. Apparently this face-saving concept has been officially accepted by the Ministerial Association of the General Conference of Seventh-day Adventists* for in their publication Seventh-day  2. Adventists Believe..., we read:

> This judgment is not for the benefit of the Godhead. It is primarily for the benefit of the universe, answering the charges of Satan and giving assurance to the unfallen creation that God will allow into His kingdom only

those who truly have been converted. So God
opens the books of record for impartial in-
spection. Dan. 7:9,10 (Seventh-day Adventists
Believe...p.325)
The issue is with God and the universe, not
between God and the true child. (Ibid p.326)

Such teaching is rank heresy and if believed,
does have the effect of taking the urgency of
the warning of the first angel away from the
individual by placing God in the "hot-seat".* 3.
This brings us closer to the beliefs of Rome and
her daughters whose teachings leave no room for
an individual investigative judgment. How can
they, when they believe that at death, the soul
has already been consigned to heaven, purgatory
or the everlasing flames of hell?
This teaching in Seventh-day Adventists
Believe... is very different from that of historic Adventism. Just listen to what the then-
president of the General Conference had to say
just thirteen years earlier (1975):

The apostle Paul declares: "We must all appear before the judgment seat of Christ that
everyone may receive the things done in his
body, according to that he hath done, whether
it be good or bad!" (2 Cor. 5:10) We may not
like it, we may not believe it, we may not be
prepared for it, but the inspired writer
declares it nonetheless certain that everyone
of us has a court case pending before the
heavenly tribunal... The great final judgment
determines in which group you and I and every
person born into this world will be - saved
or lost - when Jesus returns. Not everyone
who makes a start in the Christian way will
go through to the kingdom. 'Once in grace,
always in grace' is neither a doctrine of the

remnant church or of the scriptures. 'He that shall endure unto the end, the same shall be saved' Jesus taught. (Matthew 24:13) The judgment separates those who merely begin to serve the Lord from those who follow Him unto the end. (R.H. Pierson, We Still Believe pp. 123, 124)

**Truly, a backsliding church does lessen the distance between itself and the papacy!**

A church can apostatise in either of two ways – it can grow careless and indifferent to its special beliefs that have set it apart as a denomination; or it can revert to the beliefs and practices which it had originally discarded by assiduously promoting a deceitful campaign of subversion.

Both types of apostasy require the assistance of time and funerals. The latter type must inevitably be planned and controlled by the religious system to which its victim is attracted. We know of but one religious system which has formed a specific organisation to subvert Protestantism – the Roman Catholic Church with its misnamed "Society of Jesus".

In his book Alberto, ex-Roman Catholic priest Dr Alberto Rivera, tells how he was one of many young seminarians trained by the Jesuits to infiltrate Protestant denominations. He says:

The first Protestant groups they [Jesuits] moved on were the 7th Day Adventists [sic] and the Full Gospel Business Men. (p.28)

In a later public interview with Mike Clute, Alberto not only reaffirmed that Jesuits had penetrated the S.D.A. church but said that on a membership basis, the S.D.A. church has been infiltrated more thoroughly than any other. Not surprisingly, along with the Roman Catholic church, some evangelical-type Adventist ministers and academics have not only denied Rivera's claim, but they are known to have exercised their imagination with hilarious descriptions of Jesuits lurking in the shadows of Adventist churches and institutions. The author does not seek to gainsay such people for they probably have the advantage of varying degrees of association with Rome and her daughters.

In the following three chapters we will consider briefly aspects of the Church's conduct which appear to be consistent with that of a papal hierarchy and leave it to the reader to determine the credibility of Alberto Rivera's claims.

*1."Clayton" is a brand of non-alcoholic drink advertised in Australia as "The drink you have when you're not drinking".

*2.Seventh-day Adventists Believe...comes "with the authorisation and encouragement of President Neal C. Wilson and the other officers of the General Conference ...to furnish reliable information on the beliefs of our church" (p. V)

*3.Terminology used by G. Youlden (Avondale Memorial Church service, 20 August 1988)

# Chapter 23

# "WE STILL BELIEVE"

When Robert Pierson became General Conference president, the plan to pervert Adventist doctrine received a setback. Questions On Doctrine went out of print. LeRoy Froom had to act to salvage the situation, so he wrote the book, Movement Of Destiny under the guise of fulfilling Elder Daniells' wish that he explain to the church the meaning of righteousness by faith.

In reality, MOD turned out to be a defence of the book Questions On Doctrine which if its real purpose were known, was not likely to evoke the enthusiasm of President Pierson. Froom must have realised that it was vital to have the president's approval and recommendation for his book to have wide distribution and acceptance. So Froom had printed thousands of copies of a promotional pamphlet titled The Fascinating Story of Movement Of Destiny. In it he made great store of the fact that he was about to fulfil Elder Daniells' commission and that the Foreword to Movement Of Destiny contained a glowing recommendation by the president of the General Conference – Elder Robert Pierson. Neither was he backward in proclaiming that the vice-president, Neal C. Wilson had given a similar recommendation in his Preface.

However, after publication of Movement Of Destiny, President Pierson received a rude shock. He was reading things that he had not seen in the manuscript! His reaction was to forbid the publishers to use his Foreword in any future editions.* So when the next edition came out, Pierson's Foreword was deleted, but Elder

1.

Wilson must have agreed whole-heartedly with the book, for his Preface of approval remained.

Elder Pierson was troubled! He had been unwittingly and unfairly used. So he set about to write a book titled We Still Believe. (R & H Publishing Assoc. 1975) The very title indicates that he was aware that heresy was abroad. In it he re-affirmed the doctrines worked out by our pioneers, including our belief in Christ's continuing work of atonement in the heavenly sanctuary. Commenting on Fundamental Fourteen of the SDA Yearbook, 1973-1974 which states that "the priestly work of our Lord is the antitype of the work of the Jewish priests" he says:

> The Seventh-day Adventist Church today still believes the great truths presented in these symbols of salvation. We have neither changed our minds nor our position – **the sanctuary truth is present truth today just as it was Oct. 23,1844, when the Lord revealed it initially to Hiram Edson...**" (We Still Believe p.111)

On page 119, he quotes the Lord's messenger:

> The Sanctuary in heaven is the very centre of Christ's work on behalf of men. (Great Controversy p.488)

And again:

> The intercession of Christ in man's behalf in the sanctuary above is as essential to the plan of salvation as was His death upon the cross. (Ibid. p.489)

Then he makes crystal clear his belief that Christ's present work in the sanctuary is a continuation of the atonement by quoting from Great Controversy p. 489:

> "We are now living in the great day of atone

ment." (<u>We Still Believe</u> p. 120)

In 1978, Elder R.H. Pierson retired from the presidency of the General Conference before his term of office had expired.* During the Annual Council of the General Conference (1978) he was moved to give a farewell address in which he gave an impassioned plea for the preservation of the faith. He warned of the approaching of the omega of apostasy:

2.

> Brethren, I beg of you, study, know what is ahead, then with God's help prepare your people to meet it.

> "Regrettably" he said, "there are those in the church who belittle the inspiration of the total Bible ...who question the Spirit of Prophecy's short chronology of the earth, and who subtly and not-so-subtly attack the Spirit of Prophecy ...There are some who point to the reformers and contemporary theologians as a source and the norm for Seventh-day Adventist doctrine ...There are those who wish to forget the standards of the church we love. There are those who covet and would court the favour of the evangelicals; those who would throw off the mantle of a peculiar people; and those who would go the way of the secular, materialistic world..

> Fellow leaders, beloved brethren and sisters – don't let it happen! ...I appeal to Andrews University, to the Seminary, to Loma Linda University – don't let it happen! **We are not Seventh-day Anglicans, not Seventh-day Lutherans, we are Seventh-day Adventists! This is God's last church with God's last message!"**

*1.On the 6th October 1988, Elder Robert Pierson wrote the author: "Some portions of Elder Froom's manuscript Movement Of Destiny I had not read before its publication. Much of it I had read however, and what I read I heartily agreed with and was glad to write the requested Foreword. After reading some portions later, I declined to have my Foreword used in any subsequent editions."

*2.While it is generally believed that Elder Pierson retired for reasons of health, some who are close to the G.C. consider that he was "eased" out of the presidency. In view of his adherence to historic Adventism (as shown by his repudiation of some teachings in MOD in his book "We Still Believe", this claim appears credible.

Further, it will be noted that since his retirement, practically every one of his warnings given in his fare-well speech (see p.153) have gone unheeded; on the contrary, it seems that some curia-like body has seen to it that they have been put into practice!

# Chapter 24

# THE WASHINGTON "CURIA"

---

The Roman Curia is described as "the highly complicated and structured hierarchical body which is the Holy See's civil service" (Pontiff, p.49 by Thomas & Morgan-Witts, Granada Publishing)

Popes may come, and popes may go, but the Roman Curia, like the civil servants of an elected government need to remain in place. It is the curia which shapes and co-ordinates the political affairs of the psuedo-Christian system centred in the Vatican.

Pope John Paul I did not appreciate all the advice tendered to him by his curia. He had some plans of his own. On the thirty-third day of his pontificate, he made the decision to pull his liberal army of Jesuits back into line. He summoned the iron-willed Superior-General of that society, Pedro Arrupe, to appear before him on the following morning to answer to charges of spiritual sedition, having steered his twenty-seven thousand members "on a direct collision course with orthodox church dogma" (Ibid, p.364)

Before Pope Paul I finally retired that night he sat up in bed going over the papers that had been prepared for the Jesuit Superior. But they were not to be delivered; they were found the next morning scattered near his dead body, still sitting up in bed! (Ibid. p. 378)

It seems that the General Conference of the SDA Church has had a few men who have entrenched themselves in the administration at Washington DC. Presidents come and presidents go, but some

names appear almost as fixtures in a curia-like
band of executive directors.

While God's messenger remained in our midst,
such men were subjected to the restraining voice
of rebuke.    But after her death the papal-like
tendencies    of    the    "kingly"    government    were
nurtured and exploited by the growing hierarchy.
Soon they would take the opportunity to flex
their muscles.

Dr Benjamin G. Wilkinson was a forceful and
outspoken figure of the time. His feelings about
the exercise of "kingly" power were well known,
for along with Mrs White and Elders Waggoner and
Jones, he had, as a young worker, voted in 1903
against    the    re-institution    of    a    presidential-
type government.

The SDA Encyclopedia reveals some interesting
details    about    Wilkinson's    outstanding    career.
He    trained    for    the    ministry    at    Battle    Creek
College, became an evangelist in Wisconsin, obtained a B.A. at the University of Michigan and
returned to Battle Creek College as dean.    After
a short spell as president of the Canadian Conference, he became the Dean of Theology at Union
College.      He    is    credited    with    commencing    our
work in Rome, Paris and in Spain, having spent
four years as president of the Latin Conference
in the Southern European Division.

Returning to North America, we find him as
evangelist, Dean of Theology at Washington Missionary College and president of Columbia Union
Conference, and Kansas and East Pennsylvanian
Conferences.

In 1935 Wilkinson became president of the
Washington Missionary College, which post he
held until 1945. While in his previous position
as dean,    Dr Wilkinson perceived the trend among
Adventist scholars to favour the modern versions

of the Bible.*                                          1.

He was aware that the Pacific Press Association had published a book by William P Pierce
titled The World's Best Book (1930). This book
elevated the American Revised Version by saying
that the two thousand or more changes in the New
Testament "had done no violence to the original
sense" but had in fact, refined it (P.83). Such
a conclusion was based on the premise that since
the translation of the King James Bible, more
reliable codices had become available such as
the Alexandrian, Vatican and Sinaiatic, which
the author describes as "great Codices"(See
chapter XIII The World's Best Book)

Wilkinson knew that the ARV had done "violence to the original sense". He was aware that
these "more reliable" manuscripts carried Roman
Catholic readings of the Latin Vulgate which had
been rejected by the Protestants of the Reformation. They had been secretly injected into the
supposed revision of the Authorised Version in
1881 by the extensive use of the carefully hidden Greek New Testament of Doctors Westcott and
Hort. These clergymen of the Church of England
had long fallen under the spell of Ritualism,
Romanism and Higher Criticism. (See Our Authorized Bible Vindicated, Chapter IX).

The Revised Versions had not been generally
received with favour. Some sixty years after the
publication of the RV and twenty years after the
ARV, the popular Ladies Home Journal commented
on the virtues of the Authorised Version:

> Now, as the English-speaking people have the
> best Bible in the world...we ought to make
> the most of it...This means that we ought in-
> variably in the church and on public occa-
> sions to use the Authorized Version; all
> others are inferior. (Nov. 1921)

A few months later, the <u>Herald and Presbyter</u> magazine denounced the Revised Version:

This Revised Version is in large part in line with what is known as 'Modernism'. Those who really investigate the matter... realize that the RV is part of a movement to modernize Christian thought and faith and do away with established truth. (July 16, 1924)

Apparently Dr Wilkinson's concerns over our Church's acceptance of the ARV were not appreciated by the Washington hierarchy. General Conference president, W.A. Spicer wrote to Wilkinson expressing his concern that he or the College should make an issue of the comparative merits of Bible translations. He stated:

...When one of our leading colleges gives publicity to this matter as really a controversial issue, it is blazing a new trail. It is my conviction that none of our colleges should give public agitation to a question that involves a new issue, especially one pertaining to the Word of God, without counsel from the General Conference Committee in Council (Letter Nov.18, 1928).

But it seems that Wilkinson was by no means the only one to air his views without obtaining the sanction of the growing papal-like power in Washington. On Jan. 14, 1930, President Spicer was constrained to write to Elder W.W. Prescott, who as Signs Editor had run a series of articles on the versions. (In reality, these articles downgraded the KJV by elevating the Revised Versions):

I have just read the fourth article of the series. I must say, Brother Prescott, that I feel concerning your setting forth of the faultiness of Bible manuscripts that this is ill-timed and harmful. The tendency of this kind of discussion I believe is to spread questioning and unbelief.

But even as Spicer was showing his concern, Dr Wilkinson had been busy and by June 1930 he had written and published a book, Our Authorized Bible Vindicated. It was "written with the fervent hope that it will confirm and establish faith in God's Word, which through the ages has been preserved inviolate". (Foreword).

He then demonstrated that there were fundamentally two different Bibles – the uncorrupted and the corrupted, as represented by the Protestant Bibles and the Roman Catholic. It was the Authorized Bible of King James, which nourished the Protestant Reformation in the English-speaking world, having followed the same NT text of Erasmus as Tyndale had used in his English Bible.

Wilkinson then showed how the Jesuits had infiltrated Oxford University, and insinuated their Roman Bibles into the Revised Version in order to combat the authority of the Authorized Version which they saw as a "paper pope". Catholics gloated at the fact that this had been accomplished by the Protestants themselves. Said Cardinal Wiseman:

> When we consider the scorn cast by the Reformers upon the Vulgate (Catholic Bible), and their recurrence, in consequence to the Greek, [text of Erasmus] as the only accurate standard, we cannot but rejoice at the silent triumph which truth has at length gained over clamorous error. For, in fact, the principal writers who have avenged the Vulgate, and obtained for it its critical pre-eminence, are

Protestants." (<u>Wiseman Essays</u>, Vol.1, p.104)

Wilkinson also dealt at length with the Roman input into the American RV. He showed how Dr Philip Schaff, president of the American Committee of Revision had brought from Germany the contaminating theory of "historical development" which had filled Oxford with the Roman poison of Modernism. Wilkinson quoted (p.236):

> It is quite time that the churches of our country should awake to the extent and tendencies of this movement in the midst of American Protestantism. After a series of advances and retractions, strongly resembling the tactics of the Tractarian party [an Oxford group] in England, we have at length a bold avowal of the 'primacy of Peter', the fundamental and test doctrine of the Papacy, followed by a concision of every vital point of Christianity – Church, Ministry, Worship, Sacraments, and the right of Private Judgment to Romanism, and that too, while the name and the forms of Protestantism are (as far as possible) studiously retained.(<u>New Brunswick Review</u>, May 1854, p.20)

Wilkinson's book brought a swift response from the General Conference – but not the kind of response that Bible-believing Protestants would expect.The church that had "recognised the equal value of the Authorized and the ARV" (G.C. Committee, March 20, 1930) and had recently extolled the virtues of the ARV in <u>The World's Best Book</u>, denounced Wilkinson's book as "unauthorized". Said Vice-president J.L. McElhany in a letter to Union and Local conferences in North America:

> The book in question has not been passed upon

by a book committee of any of our publishing
houses. ...Our Authorized Bible Vindicated
can be of no particular help to our work, and
will only serve to continue the agitation of
a question which we believe should be
avoided. (Letter, July 27, 1930)

But the Washington "Curia" did not let the
matter rest. They were so concerned by
Wilkinson's exposure of the Jesuit plan to wreck
the Protestant Bible that they formed a committee to defame Our Authorized Bible Vindicated.*    2.
They came up with a document which purported
to be a review of Wilkinson's book. But for
reasons best known to themselves, no names are
appended to this document. A copy of Wilkinson's
Answers to the Reviewer's Objections is in the
author's possession.
Fortunately, Wilkinson listed each significant objection and replied to each one, so we
have a fairly accurate overview of the objections. His reply must be regarded by any impartial reader as an exposure of a gross misrepresentation of facts by a hostile Review committee. Wilkinson comments thus:
But those who wrote the document to which I
now reply were under obligation, since they
called it a "review" to be impartial and to
present the good and the strong side of my
arguments as well as those phases which
seemed to them to be weak. This they notably
failed to do. (Introduction p.1)

He then listed eight great arguments which
the Reviewers had chosen to ignore:

1. The Romanizing and Unitarian character of
Westcott and Hort, two leading English Revisers.

2. The grave charges concerning Dr Philip Schaff, President of the American Revision Committee.

3. The connection between the Revision of the AV and the Oxford movement which Jesuitized England.

4. The arguments drawn from the [RC] Council of Trent which voted among other means of combating the Reformation to "put the [RC] Vulgate on its feet".

5. That the Catholic scholars rejoiced that the RV had restored Catholic readings that had been denounced in the Reformation.

6. The argument drawn from the chapter "The Reformers Reject the Bible of the Papacy".

7. The tremendous argument drawn from the great struggle over the Jesuit Bible of 1582.

8. The chapter, "Three Hundred Years of Attack on the King James Version" by Jesuits, higher critics, and pantheistic German scholars. (From Introduction to Answers to Reviewers'Objections)

**It will be noticed that all of the above points involve the struggle for papal supremacy over Protestantism.** These the Reviewers could not deny, so they ignored them. The objections and accusations which they did raise, many of which were puerile, were ably refuted by Wilkinson. No wonder the General Conference "Curia" were anxious to bury all traces of this resounding defeat. It is reported that the General Conference requested that Wilkinson not circulate his reply to their objections. (Clute tape).

Interestingly, in later years, and currently, the denomination's attempts to justify most modern versions to the detriment of the Authorized King James Bible, ignore those same great points listed by Wilkinson. Instead, they trot out the time-worn arguments put forth by Roman Catholics and their lackeys in Protestantism. A typical example is to be found in the recent series of six articles by Arthur J. Ferch, published in the South Pacific Record, commencing 25 March 1989, titled "History of the New Testament".

Dr Benjamin G. Wilkinson was a studious man with an enquiring mind. During investigations which he had made into the history of the New Testament, he had come to realize that God's guardians of His truth through the Dark Ages were also the custodians of true scripture. This of course, is logical, and had been acknowledged by Mrs E.G. White:

> The Waldenses were among the first of the people of Europe to obtain a translation of the Holy Scriptures.
> They had the truth unadulterated, and this rendered them the special objects of hatred and persecution.
> But in a most wonderful manner it was preserved uncorrupted through all the ages of darkness.(Great Controversy, pp. 65,69)

According to a friend of the Wilkinson family, Wilkinson's ability as a scholar and researcher had come to the notice of Cordell Hull, then U.S. Secretary of State. He issued Wilkinson with credentials which virtually unlocked to him the vaults of the world, thus enabling him to examine rare historical documents and manuscripts.

In 1944, the Pacific Press Publishing Association published Wilkinson's findings in the book, Truth Triumphant. Like his previous work, Our Authorized Bible Vindicated, it was greatly appreciated by the rank and file of Adventists. Here was a book which demonstrated that the great truths of God had been safely handed down from apostolic times and guarded by His true church until present times. But it was the church in the wilderness and not the church in Rome that was the custodian of Truth!

This was a book that would strengthen the faith and beliefs of every Seventh-day Adventist. But the Washington "Curia" was not pleased. According to the Clute interview, L.E. Froom instructed the Pacific Press to destroy the plates of Truth Triumphant. This could explain why this much sought-after book has not been republished by the denomination.*

No doubt Wilkinson's exposure of the false scriptures and the role played by them in fostering apostasy had left its mark on Adventism.

In 1954, the General Conference reacted by publishing the book Problems in Translation, the work of a nameless committee. But most of the problems were in fact, brought about by the church's increasing acceptance of the modern versions. It sought to deal with the problem by trying to please everyone. After reciting the stance taken back in the early 'thirties, that the 1611 KJV and the 1901 ARV "shall serve us without discrimination..", they also appealed to our workers to co-operate "in endeavouring to preserve the unity of our people" by "leaving all free to use the version of their choice" (Problems in Translation pp. 74,75)

So once again, Wilkinson's timely warnings

3.

had been rebuffed mainly on the grounds of unity. No attempt was made to address the real issue – that it was the church in the wilderness which had been appointed as the guardians of God's Word and not Rome, and that Rome had foisted its corrupted versions upon unsuspecting Protestants and Seventh-day Adventists alike.

And then comes this remarkably contradictory statement:

> If resort is made indiscriminately to the various translations, the reader or hearer gets the impression that the different versions stand on an equal footing, as far as authoritatively transmitting the word of God is concerned, which is not the case. (Ibid P.57).

(Such a foray into the minefields of consensus must have been deemed successful, for the Seventh-day Adventist church has since come to rely increasingly on consensus statements.)

But the time was not far off when the church would drop all pretence of caution, and impartiality. They would not only foist the Roman Bibles on their own membership, but would become foremost in recommending them to Christendom at large. In short, they would become "Rome's Little Helper". But that is another story to be told in the following chapter.

In retrospect, the decade of the 'fifties must be seen as a great watershed in Seventh-day Adventist history. By 1954, Elder R.R.Figuhr had assumed the presidency of the General Conference. He was fresh from associate editorship of the Ministry magazine with Elder R.A. Anderson who in turn had been an Associate Editor with L.E. Froom. Circumstances were now favourable for the great leap (backward) into apostasy. We have seen how this was accomplished with the help of the evangelicals, Dr Barnhouse and Walter Martin.

Before long, an event took place which President Figuhr saw as a distinct threat to the "Curia's" plans. A book, titled The Living Witness, consisting of forty-seven "significant articles" culled from the Signs of the Times, was published by the Pacific Press Publishing Association in 1959. When Elder Figuhr read it, he reacted with alacrity. Here was a book, published within two years of Questions On Doctrine which contradicted the "completed atonement". What would Barnhouse and Martin say? What would our new-found friends in Christendom think?

The offending article was written by the late Elder James White, Editor of the 'Signs':

(Jesus Christ) ascended on high to be our only mediator in the Sanctuary in heaven where, with His own blood, He makes atonement for our sins; which atonement, so far from being made at the cross, which was but the offering of the sacrifice, is the very last portion of His work as priest, according to the example of the Levitical priesthood which foreshadowed and prefigured the ministry of our Lord in heaven.(The Living Witness, p.2)

We are indebted to Elder M.L. Andreasen for the following account of Figuhr's reaction:

When Elder Figuhr read the statement in the "Living Witness" that the atonement was not made on the cross, he ordered the books that had already been bound destroyed. Several hundred books that had already been shipped out, were also destroyed, as well as 2000 signatures that had not yet been bound. The financial loss would be worthwhile... It was

necessary that a whole signature of 16 pages
be replaced with corrected material.  (M.L.
Andreasen's Letters to the Churches)

Andreasen continued with this highly significant statement:

If the question was raised why a discussion
should arise as to where and when the atonement was made, Elder White would answer: "On
this question hangs the existence of the SDA
denomination.  If the atonement was made on
the cross in 31 A.D. and this atonement was
complete, perfect, final as the Ministry
asserts, then there cannot possibly be another final atonement 1810 years later.  And
if there is no day of atonement at the end of
the 2300 days in 1844, then the whole 1844
movement was a mistake, and the Adventists
false prophets.  If there was no cleansing of
the sanctuary in 1844, then the Three Angels'
Messages and the Hour of Judgment call were a
false alarm, and then we may as well 'totally
repudiate' our entire message as the evangelicals state our leaders have done and which
the leaders have never denied.(Ibid.)

(Both quotations, as reprinted in the M.L.
Andreasen File, p.96, by Laymen Ministry News,
1988)

Surely it would be difficult to imagine an
action more closely aligned with papal-like
behaviour! Its exposure by Andreasen in his
Letters to the Churches helps us to understand
why the "Curia" sought revenge by depriving him
of his credentials and his sustentation.

And so today, when we turn to the book The
Living Witness, we find that the 'Witness' has
been maimed.  The dagger struck and His message

has been muted. We may well ask:

**Which church has a vested interest in abolishing Christ's mediatorial role between God and man, if it is not the church of Rome? Which church would want to replace the Bible which brought on the Protestant Reformation and from which we obtained our doctrines?**

**Is Alberto's claim that the Jesuits have successfully infiltrated Adventism really so incredible?**

**Why should Rome not take advantage of a system with which they are familiar already? — the papal-like system that A.T. Jones had already identified as that already adopted by the Seventh-day Adventist Church!**

*1. This is not surprising as, in 1926, the Berrien Springs College Press published a text book on doctrines for use in S.D.A. colleges, in which it claimed the ARV to be "more accurate, more scholarly, more valuable" than the AV (p.59)

*2. As usual, the members of the Committee remain anonymous. But the names L.E. Froom, L.E. Howell, and M.E.Kern are currently connected with this committee. It is interesting to note that when the AV was presented in The World's Best Book as having inferior manuscripts to the ARV, the "Curia" showed no concern!

*3. The author understands that Truth Triumphant is now available from:- Leaves-Of-Autumn Books Incorporated
P.O. Box 440 Payson, AZ. 85547 USA

# CHAPTER 25

# ROME'S LITTLE HELPER

---

By the end of Elder Figuhr's term as G.C. president, some of the modern Bible versions had become highly popular with many Adventist scholars and writers. The N.T. Greek of Westcott and Hort had long become the authoritative text in our colleges. The writer recalls that this was the Greek N.T. used in the training of ministers at the Australasian Missionary College (now Avondale College) as far back as 1937.

Consequently, when a question arose over a controversial text in the modern versions, the Jesuit corrupted text of Westcott and Hort from which most modern versions derive, was appealed to as the arbiter! Such fallacious reasoning is commonly used to this day.

But it appears that the Washington "Curia" was not content to rest on its laurels. There was a whole wide world of Christendom out there and it was lagging behind, burdened with the "archaic" Bible of King James.

Elder R.H. Pierson succeeded Elder Figuhr as G.C. President. Although he was considered to be conservative and fundamental it was perceived that in his writings he was an enthusiastic supporter of modern versions. [Later, in his book, We Still Believe (1975) we witness the anomaly of a "Defender of the Faith" having to gain permission to use scripture from the owners of four modern versions!]

So in 1969, the SDA church seriously launched its career as Rome's Little Helper per medium of their public outreach journal, Signs of the Times (May 1969). The question, "Can We Trust

Modern Bible Versions?"* was answered by A. 1.
Graham Maxwell:

> You can trust the modern versions.  Read as
> many as you can.  (p.31)

Unfortunately, Maxwell seeks to instil trust
in the modern versions by denigrating the Authorized Version to the status of a "revision".  He
calls it the "1611 revision". But it is apparent
that the translators of the AV would not appreciate Maxwell's designation, for they regarded
their work as a translation. Read their offering
to the "Most high and mighty Prince James":

> ...that out of the Original Sacred Tongues,
> together with comparing of the labours, both
> in our own, and other foreign languages of
> many worthy men who went before us, there
> should be one more exact translation of the
> holy Scriptures into the English tongue.

As for the Revised Version, it is claimed
that it is dishonestly named, for it is not a
revision of the KJV.  It was supposed to be, and
it is claimed to be, but the fraud was quickly
exposed by Dr John William Burgon, Dean of
Chichester.  He comments on the New Testament:

> The English (as well as the Greek) is hope-
> lessly at fault... But the "Revised Version"
> is inaccurate as well; exhibits defective
> scholarship, I mean in countless places.
> It is however, the systematic depravation of
> the underlying Greek which does so grievously
> offend me; for this is nothing else but a
> poisoning of the River of Life at its sacred
> source. (Dedication to Revision Revised, 1883
> p.VI)

Burgon comments  further on the  injection of

the underlying Greek text of Westcott and Hort
(as opposed to the Greek text of Erasmus used by
the King James translators):

> For if the underlying Greek text be mistaken,
> what else but incorrect must the English
> translation be... To my surprise and annoy-
> ance, it (RV) proved to be a New Translation
> rather than a Revision of the Old... (Ibid.
> Preface p.XII)

Bible teacher, J.J. Ray simply shows the fal-
lacy of Maxwell's argument:

> The Revision of 1881, the American Standard
> Version of 1901, the Revised Standard Ver-
> sion, the Amplified, Expanded and Paraphrased
> Bibles are in no true sense a revision of the
> King James of 1611.  If they were, they would
> follow the same Greek Text, the Textus Recep-
> tus.  All that they should have done, was to
> replace the obsolete words, (etc...) Instead
> of doing this, the Revision Committee yielded
> to human arguments, and permitted the new
> radical changes to be secretly forced upon
> them. (God Wrote Only One Bible p.30.)

It is also sad to note the pathetic attempt
by Maxwell to invest the RV and the ARV (1901)
with the aura of "authorization", describing the
latter as the fifth "Authorized Version" of the
English Bible.

It must be obvious to God-fearing Christians
that the only truly Authorized Bible is that
which was given by God to man.  The King James
Bible has become known as the Authorized Bible
simply because it was commissioned by royal
decree... But to call the ARV an authorized
Bible is incredible for it was authorised by
none other than those who financed the venture

and kept the American cash registers ringing. As for the RSV, which claims to be a revision of the ASV, it was authorised by vote of the National Council of Churches of Christ! (Preface to RSV, p.IV)

Such semantic adventures by Maxwell can only be regarded as a strained association of ideas calculated to present the modern versions as healthy descendants of the KJV.

But interestingly, Maxwell's claim is also refuted by none other than the translators of one of the modern versions which he recommends:

> The Revised Version, which appeared in 1881, makes a new departure, especially in that it abandoned the so-called Received Text, (Erasmus) which has reigned ever since prin-ted editions of the New Testament began. (Introduction to NEB, New Testament)

And, as if to put the lid on Maxwell's spe-cious argument, we read this astounding admis-sion in the New KJV:

> ...a growing number of scholars now regard the Received Text far more reliable than previously thought... The New King James New testament has been based on this Received Text, thus perpetuating the tradition begun by William Tyndale in 1525 and continued by the 1611 translators in rendering the Author-ized Version    (Preface).

Wilkinson's contention that his Reviewers had failed to acknowledge the corrupted stream of Romanism in the new versions is still valid today.   Certain influential people in the SDA organization prefer to promote Constantine's illegitimate offspring of church and state. The aforementioned series of articles  by A.J. Ferch in the <u>South Pacific Record</u> (1989) is an example.

Among the various Bible Societies is one based in the United Kingdom known as the Trinitarian Bible Society. New testaments based on the Greek New Testament of Westcott and Hort are notorious for their degradation of Christ's divinity. Therefore, the Trinitarian Bible Society promote and distribute only Bibles based on the Received Text, the most shining example 'of which is the KJV. This is in stark contrast to the various national Bible Societies which come under the umbrella of the United Bible Societies (UBS) and under the spell of Rome. The SDA church has long since become one of UBS's loyal supporters.

The United Bible Societies are very active in translating Scripture into various languages. Mostly they are ecumenical projects which produce inter-confessional Bibles. The October 1985 quarterly Record of the Trinitarian Tract Society sheds some interesting information on ecumenism which involves the SDA church:

> The work of the Bible Society (UBS) acquired a new dimension with the setting up of a conservative committee made up of three representatives from the Roman Catholic, the Anglican and the Seventh-day Adventist churches. This committee will supervise the translation reproduction and distribution in the Seychelles. (UBS Report, 1984)

Monsignor Alberto Ablondi, who in 1985 was an executive member of the European Regional Executive of the UBS, sees these ecumenical projects as "one of the most important advancements of post Vatican II ecumenism – an important step towards unity" (Ward-Event No. 57, p.6, 1984).

As interconfessional Bibles must of necessity be of the variety acceptable to Rome and her Babylonian daughters, and in view of Adventism's newly-demonstrated preference for Roman corruptions of Scripture, surely it is correct to assume that the SDA denomination has now joined with Rome in their Jesuit-inspired plan to produce as well as to disseminate Bibles of Anti-Christ.

But the "Curia" of Washington has gone much further than this. They are now foisting Rome's Bibles upon their hapless Adventist church members by the mandatory use of the Seventh-day Adventist Hymnal (1985).

This hymn book contains a section of responsive Scripture Readings for corporate worship, together with a selection of canticles and prayers. They are taken from eight Bible versions. From the following table it will be seen that our official hymn book denigrates the Protestant Bible of our pioneers to a minor position amongst the versions used. The Roman Catholic Jerusalem Bible is used over two and a half times more frequently than the KJV!

| | |
|---|---|
| The NIV | used 68 times |
| The Jerusalem Bible | used 38 times |
| The NKJV | used 34 times |
| The RSV | used 28 times |
| The NEB | used 22 times |
| The TEV | used 15 times |
| The KJV | used 14 times |
| The NASB | used 3 times |

So, by this Trojan-horse device, people who normally would use only the KJV are placed in a position where the pastor can manoeuvre them into reading from the new versions.

Dr Alberto Rivera, who claims to have been trained by the Jesuits to infiltrate Protestant churches, has written a booklet, Sabotage, explaining the Jesuit plan to subvert Protestanism by the use of Roman-tainted Bibles. He says:

In the last eighty years we've had about eighty-one new English Bibles (all Roman Catholic) based on Origen's corrupted text, all trying to push the King James Bible out of the picture. Soon there will be an ecumenical bible (one common bible for all religions) preparing the way for the anti-Christ. (Sabotage 1979 p.29)

Predictably, the Roman Catholic church denies Rivera's priestly training. But surprisingly, many SDAs join with apostate Protestantism in slavishly repeating Rome's denials! In so doing they indicate their refusal to recognise the role of Jesuits as destroyers of Protestantism. But more particularly, such denials are designed to protect versions of the Bible which are seen as providing a semblance of authority for the teachings of apostate Adventism.

Of particular interest is the trans-denominational popularity of the NIV. Its meteoric rise to favour with SDA educators, writers and pastors, and as we have just seen, its overwhelming predominance among the scripture readings of the SDA Church Hymnal, is nothing short of phenomenal.

Undoubtedly, this is the ecumenical Bible to which Dr Rivera referred as "preparing the way for anti-christ". (It is available in most R.C. bookshops.) As we consider the doctrines so destructive to Adventism as discussed in the two-pronged dagger aimed at the heart of Adventism, can an honest Seventh-day Adventist deny the truth of Rivera's prediction?

As we note the insinuation into the SDA Church of doctrines favourable to Rome, we marvel at the fervour and dedication with which the Washington "Curia" has expedited the Roman plan to replace the Protestant Bible of King James with their own corrupted bibles. Such actions would be entirely consistent with a Jesuit-controlled church. But if Rivera's claim of Jesuit infiltration is incorrect, then surely it is reasonable to conclude that certain people in the Adventist "Curia" are every bit as competent, and dedicated in the work of Roman subversion as the Jesuits themselves!

But there remains another powerful witness to the Church's desire to emulate Rome. It is the confessions and actions of leadership itself which conform to A.T. Jones' description of a "kingly ruling" church power:-

**The Seventh-day Adventist denomination is more like the Catholic Church than is any other Protestant church in the world.** (See Chapter 13, p.73)

As the year 1974 drew to its close, the General Conference found itself in a United States District court as the defendent in a lawsuit brought against the Pacific Press Publishing Association (PPPA) by the Equal Employment Opportunity Commission (EEOC) of the United States.

The case centred on the PPPA'S treatment of two of its female employees - one a secretary to the editor of the Signs of the Times, the other an editorial assistant to the Book Editor. It appears that the Church's treatment of these people in pecuniary matters fell considerably short of what was considered fair and equitable by the EEOC.

For the purpose of this chapter, we will not concern ourselves with the rights and wrongs of the case, but rather we shall note the tactics of the General Conference, through its Brief, in its desire to successfully contest the suit.

The opening Brief sought to confuse the real issue by claiming that this was "a head-on confrontation between church and state" and that the Government was seeking "an injunction which would control the affairs of the Church and dictate the manner in which the Church carries on God's work: (CIV NO.74-2025 CBR, Opening Brief.)

This, Brief saw as a violation of the First Amendment to the U.S. constitution, **and as the General Conference was the Church, it should be above all laws of the land.** In describing the meaning of the term "General Conference" it was said to have three overlapping meanings:

a. The embodiment of the Remnant Church as a Christian denomination.

b. The actual quadrennial meeting of delegates, which body alone has authority to alter Church structure in doctrine or organization.

c. The permanent staff at world headquarters in Washington DC which, acting through the executive Committee, attends to the Church work between quadrennial conferences. (Ibid)

So we see that the Washington headquarters staff takes upon itself the status of 'the church'. The Brief described Elder R.H. Pierson, President of the G.C. as "the first minister" of the SDA CHurch, while Elder Neal C. Wilson, Vice-President for North America, described himself as "the spiritual leader" of SDA's in North America. (Ibid)

For the purpose of defending the suit, it ap-

pears that Brief for the defendants sought to
establish the supreme authority of the General
Conference in the organisational structure of
the Church:

> The plain and undeniable fact is that the
> Seventh-day Adventist Church is most assur-
> edly not a 'congregational one'... but it is
> clearly of the "representative" or "hierar-
> chical" variety. (Reply Brief for Defendants
> 74-2025 CBR)

But it will be noted that a "hierarchical
variety" of church government is akin to the
Roman Catholic variety, where the "spiritual
leader" of the church also is a man! It is not
surprising then that Brief sought to categorise
the two female employees as nuns, and by implication, they should be happy to receive whatever
reward the hierarchy saw fit to pay them. This
is borne out in Neal C. Wilson's affidavit where
he quoted from the North American Division's
Working Policy, p.36:

> They [employees] shall never appeal to any
> court of law for redress from such adjust-
> ments as may be made by the denomination
> concerning any personal claim they may make.
> (Affidavit of Neal C Wilson 74-2025 CBR)

So it was pointed out that one employee had
attained a status of a licensed missionary of
the Church and the other, a credentialed missionary which, according to Brief, made her a
"minister of the Church". Therefore:

> Those who work for the Seventh-day Adventist
> Church respond to a religious vocation in
> exactly the same sense as does a cloistered
> nun.(Ibid)

But it is evident that the two ladies, both of whom were married, had a decidedly different view of their relationship to their employer. This, Elder Wilson saw as their main problem:

> The primary reason for the conflict is that these workers in the Church have been unwilling to recognize and accept the authority of the Church in determining internal policies governing the ecclesiastical nature and mission of their employing organization. (Affidavit of Neal C Wilson 74-2025 CBR)

Lest such authority appear to show papal-like overtones in defiance of state laws, Wilson closed his affidavit by revealing his source of authority:

> Finally, being conscious of the full weight and burden of my responsibilities as the spiritual leader of approximately one-half million souls, it is my duty to God and to my church to re-affirm that, with all respect and veneration for the secular laws of the United States of America duly and justly realized and rendered, we the Church owe and must render our first obedience and service to the Divine Law of Jesus Christ that the will of God may be done "on earth as it is in heaven"; and this we solemnly and reverently do, even should the carrying out of our sacred obligations result, in the words of St Paul to the Corinthians (2 Corithians 6:4,5 [RSV] "in afflictions, hardships, calamities, beatings, imprisonments".* (Sworn 27th day of 2. Nov. 1974 and signed, Neal C. Wilson)

In his affidavit, President R.H. Pierson described himself as "an ordained minister of the Gospel and president of the General Conference of Seventh-day Adventists, which is the Seventh-day Adventist church..." He stated that he was its "first minister for the time being", and proceeded to outline the order of hierarchy:

> The orders of ministers in the Seventh-day Adventist Church include ordained Ministers, credentialed Missionaries, licensed Ministers licensed Missionaries, and credentialed literature Evangelists (Affidavit of Robert H Pierson, No. 74-2025 CBR)

Elder Pierson explained:

> All denominational employees in the Seventh-day Adventist Church are regarded as church workers placed in one of two harmonious categories and designated as ministers or missionaries" (Ibid.)

But one of the interveners, Lorna Tobler, who was employed as an editorial secretary found such claims very extravagant. During her twenty-five years of connection with Adventist related institutions she had never been called a pastor or elder, never been ordained, performed a baptismal or marriage ceremony or presided at the Lord's Supper.

In spite of her considerable denominational experience, and that she was married to an Adventist minister, she had never heard or seen the term "first minister" applied to a General Conference president:

> I have frequently heard the term 'hierarchy' used among Adventists when reference is made to the Roman Catholic System, of which I have always been taught that Adventists strongly disapprove... I have never heard of Adventist Religious 'orders' or 'orders of ministry...' among Adventists, I have always heard this

term used to apply to Roman Catholicism,
which I have been taught to reject. I have
never heard any employee of Adventist-related
institutions, or any Seventh-day Adventist at
all, compared to 'a cloistered nun' and believe that such concept to be alien to Adventist thought and practice... I have never
heard any belief that everything Adventist
ministers or administrators do is 'sacra-
mental'...I have never heard it said among
Adventists that the church claims exemption
from all civil laws" (Sworn on Feb. 18, 1975
by Lorna Tobler).

In the Reply Brief for Defendants appears a
startling but significant statement which probably indicates the underlying philosophy behind
present attitudes manifested in the Seventh-day
Adventist Church:

**Although it is true that there was a period
in the life of the Seventh-day Adventist
Church when the denomination took a distinctly anti-Roman Catholic viewpoint, and the
term "hierarchy" was used in a perjorative
[depreciatory] sense to refer to the papal
form of church governance, that attitude on
the church's part was nothing more than a
manifestation of widespread anti-popery among
conservative protestant denominations in the
early part of this century and the latter
part of the last, and which has now been
consigned to the historical trash heap so far
as the Seventh-day Adventist Church is concerned.**

So there we have the witness of modern day
leadership in the Seventh-day Adventist Church.
When the  chips were down and the  dollar signs

were up, the truth came out. The Adventist
"Curia" showed its true colours and the banner
of Protestantism was trampled in the rush to
deny the message of the third angel.What would
our prophet have to say about such crass
apostasy?
Thank you for the warning Dr Rivera, but it came
too late. The 'wonderers after the beast' already appear to be well and truly in control.

*1.This article, "Can We Trust the Modern Versions?" must
   have been regarded as a masterpiece by successive
   admirers of Roman inventiveness for it has occasionally
   reappeared in Adventist publications, e.g. Adventist
   Review Nov. 1985.
*2.Many in the Seventh-day Adventist Church,especially those
   in Hungary, must wonder what happened to our President's
   solemn resolve to render first obedience to God amid
   "afflictions, hardships, calamities, beatings, imprison-
   ments".

# Chapter 26

# "A NEW ORDER"

---

**"And when these things begin to come to pass, then look up, and lift up your heads; for your redemption draweth nigh." Luke 21:28.**

As our tired world staggers towards its rendezvous with the twenty-first century A.D., we are reminded that some day along the way, we shall probably silently slip into earth's seventh millennium of history. To some, the notion that the seventh millennium should coincide with a millennium spent in Paradise, is so appealing as to make it a desired expectation.

Certainly we have lived to see the day when the world can be seen to have waxed old as a garment. (Ps. 102:26) Man's insatiable quest to improve his standard of living has brought us to the place where the very oxygen needed to sustain life is running out. His success in some areas of planet earth is causing him to flounder in his own garbage.

We have societies where people battle with their appetite in order to reduce weight, yet a large section of the world's population rarely experience the sensation of a full stomach! They are the main contributors to a population explosion!

In practically every field of man's endeavour, we find conditions that seem to indicate a fast-approaching climax. For instance: how long can the moral depravity of man continue to worsen before civilization as we know it becomes no longer tenable? With the vast build up of nuclear and biological weapons and the technology with which to deliver them to any point on earth; with the continuing breakdown of law and order through corruption of traditional law-enforcement agencies, a scenario develops that could plunge part or all of the world into utter chaos. This has happened in limited regions of the world with increasing frequency over the latter half of this century.

When we look at the world's financial affairs, we see a situation where, in spite of all the post-war plans to bring about equity among nations, the have-nots have slipped further into debt, while others have reached a state of prosperity rarely seen in earth's history. Yet today, some previously prosperous nations have reached a situation where they can no longer service their debts, let alone reduce their principal borrowings.

In the past, such were the ingredients of which wars were made. How long before man's fear of an exterminating war is overcome by his perceived need for greater wealth? From whatever viewpoint we look upon man's modern dilemma, all roads seem to be leading towards an inevitable climax – a situation where we are nearing the end of the line. And all lines seem to be converging towards the close of the twentieth century!

The apostle Paul had forseen some of the perils of the last days. He lists their causes for posterity:

For men shall be lovers of their own selves, covetous, boasters, proud ... (2 Tim. 3:1,2)

As he continues in succeeding verses he outlines the characteristics of those who have a form of godliness, but deny the power thereof. That's right. He is talking about people who profess to be followers of God! They're an unthankful and unholy lot, some are false accusers and think nothing of breaking their word. They are fierce people who actually despise those who are good. Some have even lost all natural affection! Paul is not talking about a bunch of ignoramuses. Not at all! Some are highly intellectual. They have degrees from the top universities. They are "ever learning" he says, yet "never able to come to the knowledge of the truth" (v. 7)

What a tragedy! Yet, we are told that there will be some who will not be deceived. They are those who continue in the things that they have learned from the Holy Scriptures - the things "which are able to make us wise unto salvation through faith which is in Christ Jesus" (v.15)

Particularly in Western society, do we see Paul's predictions as reality. Here are civilisations where laws are based on the Judeo-Christian ethics. They have prospered as a result of the Protestant Reformation and its attitude to work. They have arrived! So countries like Australia don't need Christianity any more. Australia has been removed from the United Nations's list of Christian countries! Just contemplate that! We have discarded the very foundation on which our society and prosperity have been built. No wonder politicians have described Australia's course as leading to a "Banana Republic"!

But just as Western society is suffering because of its abandonment of true Protestantism, so the Seventh-day Adventist Church, to whom the flickering torch of Protestantism was handed, is sliding back into the arms of Rome. It is called apostate Adventism. Think about it, dear reader **- the heresies propounded by our leadership find**

**favour in the eyes of Rome;** every suspect and corrupt practice followed by our leadership harks back to a type of organisation described by A.T. Jones as "papal-like", and the methods used to promote and enforce such practices are the methods of popery.* Instead of preaching the message of 1844 and calling people to come out of Babylon (Roman error) and prepare for the judgment, we appear determined to be counted with Babylon!

1.

Loyal Adventists will recognise these signs as those which must precede the return of Christ. They could not appear until after the close of the last great time prophecy as outlined by Daniel the prophet which culminated in the commencement of the investigative judgment in 1844, for it was upon the discovery of this great truth that the remnant church was founded.

Our situation was foretold by John in the Revelation of Jesus Christ; "And the dragon was wroth with the woman, and went to make war with the remnant of her seed, which keep the commandments of God and have the testimony of Jesus Christ." (Rev. 12:17)

Which is the church that has traditionally claimed to be the remnant? Which advocates the keeping of all the Decalogue and has the testimony of Jesus in the manifestation of the Spirit of Prophecy? Only one church has ever made this claim – the Seventh-day Adventist church.

But John tells that "the dragon [Satan] was wroth with the woman, and went to make war with the remnant of her seed, which keep the commandments of God and have the testimony of Jesus Christ". Today, having failed in his attacks from outside the Adventist denomination, Satan is attacking from within. He can do this quite easily because he has successfully insinuated a type of organisation into the Seventh-day Adventist Church that is geared to meet the demands of a papal-like government as defined by A.T. Jones. It happened in 1903 when, against the wishes of the church's prophet, A.G. Daniells allowed himself to be elected as president of a church government by men and for men.

This followed hard on the heels of the leaders' rejection of the 1888 message of righteousness by faith, which, although they may not have realized it, was probably the rejection of Jesus Christ as the head of the Seventh-day Adventist church.

And so our leaders plunged headlong into a behavioural pattern that to this very day, continues to vindicate Mrs E.G.White as a true seer of God. Listen to her predictions and see how they have come to pass:

A new organization would be established. Books of a new order would be written. A system of intellectual philosophy would be introduced. (Selected Messages Vol. 1, p.204)

"A new order" has certainly been promoted with the publication of books like Questions On Doctrine and Movement of Destiny. They have ushered in a new order based on the intellectual philosophy of men who wish to meet the requirements of apostate Protestantism.

And what of the General Conference's latest official pronouncement on our doctrines? Seventh Day Adventists Believe..." - a book written and published under the patronage of world president, Neal C. Wilson.Is it a book of a new order as predicted by our prophet?

In some respects, this book is a more subtle attack on our 1844 sanctuary message than its predecessors. As previously mentioned, it is a

consensus explanation of a consensus statement
on our fundamental beliefs! But as also pointed
out, it goes further than previous books in
drawing the logical conclusion that if the
atonement was completed at the cross, then "the
penitent believer can trust in this finished
work of our Lord". (Seventh-day Adventists
Believe..." p.315)

This then, makes an investigative judgment
completely redundant; but this book is not
honest enough to come out and openly deny the
judgment that started in 1844. It tries to get
around it by removing the professed followers of
God as the subject of the judgment and, to use
the expression of one Adventist minister, puts
God in the "hot-seat". It claims: "The issue is
with God and the universe, not between God and
the true child" (Ibid. p.326) But as we have
already noted, this goes against the historic
beliefs of Adventism and the inspired writings
as shown in the SDA Bible Commentary.

And what of Mrs White's claim of the introduction of a system of intellectual philosophy?
As with the modern Sabbath School Quarterlies,
Seventh-day Adventists Believe..." quotes
extensively from non-Adventist theologians along
with the Spirit of Prophecy as though all were
equally authoritative. God's messenger was awake
to such a ploy:

> There are men among us in responsible
> positions who hold that the opinions of a few
> conceited philosophers so-called, are more to
> be trusted than the truth of the Bible or the
> Testimonies of the Holy Spirit. (5 T p.79)

One theologian in question is the late Dr
B.F. Westcott. On page 48, he is quoted in an
attempt to explain the nature of Christ during

His incarnation. Again he is cited on page 320 as an authority on the cleansing of the heavenly sanctuary.

Now, for our purpose, we are not much interested in what Westcott believed on Christ's nature, or on the sanctuary service either. It is the fact that our Ministerial Department of the General Conference regards his credentials as befitting him (and his ilk) to instruct us on Adventist beliefs.

Dr B.F. Westcott and his colleague, Dr Hort, were the two Cambridge professors who secretly produced a Greek New Testament based largely on the Roman Vaticanus and the Sinaiticus. They secretly led the team of "revisers" of the Authorized Version to accept their New Testament, so that instead of ending up with a revision of the KJV, Protestantism was lumbered with a new translation and a Roman Catholic inspired Bible (See Chapter 25, p.170) Said Dr John W. Burgon, Dean of Chichester, in his Revision Revised concerning the revisers:

**Our Revisers ...stand convicted of having deliberately rejected the words of Inspiration in every page, and of having substituted for them fabricated Readings which the Church has long since refused to acknowledge, or else has rejected with abhorrence and which only survive at this time in a little handful of documents of the most depraved type. (Dedication p. VI, VII, 1883)**

It is not surprising that Westcott, although professing to be a Church of England clergyman, should lumber Protestantism with a Roman Catholic Bible for he was already an ardent admirer of Romanism! In 1847 he wrote from France to his fiancée describing his idolatrous visit to a

Roman Catholic monastery:

> Fortunately we found the door open. It is very small, with one kneeling place; and behind a screen was a 'Pieta' [statue of the Virgin Mary and dead Christ] the size of life . Had I been alone I could have knelt there for hours. (Life of Westcott, Vol.1, p.81)

While writing to the Archbishop of Canterbury on March 4, 1890, Westcott commented:

> No one now, I suppose, holds that the first three chapters of Genesis, for example, give a literal history. (Ibid. Vol. 2, p.69.)

It is no wonder that he displayed little inhibition when tampering with the scriptures when he was able to write:

> The battle of the inspiration of scripture is yet to be fought. (Ibid. Vol.1, p.94)

The authors of Seventh-day Adventists Believe... then call on Dr F.F.Bruce to help explain Christ's nature. (p.48) This is the man under whom Desmond Ford studied theology at Manchester University. He is reputed to follow the Plymouth Brethren persuasion, and his system of prophetic interpretation lets the Roman Catholics off the 'beastly' hook of Revelation 13. In his Foreword to Ford's book Daniel, Bruce says:

> The gospel which he [Ford] proclaims is the Gospel which I acknowledge; may it continue to speed on and triumph.

But that's not by any means all the non-Adventist theologians who are called upon to confuse us on the nature of Christ.

It is difficult to find out from Seventh-day

<u>Adventists Believe...</u> just what SDAs do believe or even are supposed to believe! Dr R. Larson claims that this book is now teaching the post lapsarian nature (<u>Our Firm Foundation</u> Sept. 1988) while S.R. Buckley claims it is teaching holy flesh. (<u>Omega of Apostasy</u> p.7)*

2.

The historic SDA biblical position could easily have been made clear by quoting a few strong statements from the Bible and the Spirit of Prophecy e.g. Rom. 8:3; Heb. 2:16,17; Heb. 4:15; DA pp.49, 112, 117).

Now, they call on Dr Philip Schaff to throw in his ideas (p.48). This is the man who brought his "historical development" theory from Europe to America and which gave rise to what became known as the "Mercersburg Movement" - seen by some as a counterpart of the Oxford Movement in England. It was seen by the <u>New Brunswick Review</u>, May 1954, as a defence of <u>Romanism</u> and an attack on American Protestantism. (See Chapter 24) In short, the authors of <u>Seventh-day Adventists Believe...</u> seem to find it prudent to use the thoughts of another Protestant traitor in an effort to aid their cause.

Yes friends, we are talking about the books of which Mrs White warned—the "books of a new order" based on a "system of intellectual philosophy". It is produced, recommended and distributed by a type of government resembling that "new order type" which God's prophet condemned.

It is this type of organisation which has been allowed to remain in place since 1903 which has continued to restrain the out-pouring of the latter rain and delay the consequent return in glory of our Lord and Saviour, Jesus Christ. The futility of such a form of government was a foregone conclusion in view of the dire consequences predicted by Mrs E.G.White back in 1904:

The enemy of souls has sought to bring in the supposition that a great reformation was to take place among Seventh-day Adventists, and that this reformation would consist in giving up the doctrines which stand as the pillars of our faith, and engaging in a process of re-organization. (Selected Messages, Vol.1, p.204)

Although God's anointed specifically mentioned the attack on our sanctuary doctrine and the messages of the three angels of Revelation 14, she also indicated that such messages vital to Adventism would not be lost:

We are God's commandment-keeping people. For the past fifty years every phase of heresy has been brought to bear upon us, to becloud our minds regarding the teaching of the Word - especially concerning the ministration of Christ in the heavenly sanctuary, and the message of Heaven for these last days, as given by the angels of the fourteenth chapter of Revelation. Messages of every order and kind have been urged upon Seventh-day Adventists, to take the place of the truth which, point by point, has been sought out by prayerful study, and testified to by the miracle-working power of the Lord. **But the waymarks which have made us what we are, are to be preserved, and they will be preserved, as God has signified through His Word and the testimony of His Spirit. He calls upon us to hold firmly, with the grip of faith, to the fundamental principles that are based upon unquestionable authority.** (Selected Messages, Vol 1, p.208)

How encouraging  then, to know that the great

prophetic truths entrusted to God's remnant
church are to be preserved! Our leaders may
fail, but God's truth will prevail. Does this
not suggest that God's truth will triumph without the present type of government which has
been in place since 1903? Our church's acknowledged authority on its sanctuary doctrine,
Elder M.L. Andreasen, thought so back in the
fifties:

> This denomination needs to go back to the
> instruction given in 1888, which was scorned.
> **We need a reform in organization that will
> not permit a few men to direct every move
> made anywhere in the world...**
> We need a reformation and revival most of
> all. If our leaders will not lead in this
> then shall there enlargement and deliverance
> arise to the Jews from another place. Esther
> 4:14 (Andreasen, <u>Letters to the Churches</u> No.
> 6)

*1.Some half-century later, Andreasen concurred with Jones:
"Here I was, for fifty years an honored member of the
church, having held responsible positions. But if I
dared hold 'views divergent from that of the responsible
leadership of the denomination', I became a member of the
'wild-eyed irresponsibles' who constituted the 'lunatic
fringe' of the denomination; and without a hearing I was
ordered to cease my activity or feel the 'brakes' applied
...**Rome went but little further.**" (<u>Letters to the
Churches</u>, No 4.)

*2.It is apparent that the authors of <u>SDAs Believe...</u> have
moved away from the dogmatic position taken in <u>QOD</u> and
<u>MOD</u> that Christ took the unfallen nature of Adam. The
author takes the view that after such indisputable evidence as recently given by R. Larson, D. Priebe and L.B.
Kostenko, upholding the "fallen nature", thinking students would hesitate to put their credibility on the line

by appearing to refute them.

Yet, if SDAs Believe... were to come out for the "fallen nature" the very basis of apostate Adventism would be removed, and the credibility of those who recommended and upheld Froom's work would suffer. Hence the obfuscation.   As N.C. Wilson was the chairman of the Guiding Committee for MOD and highly recommended the book in his Preface, and is given credit for authorising and encouraging the Ministerial Association to produce SDAs Believe... (p.v) we can see the predicament in which such people find themselves.

# CHAPTER 27

# EIGHTEEN FORTY-FOUR TO EVERMORE

**"Let us hear the conclusion of the whole matter: Fear God and keep his commandments: for this is the whole duty of man." Eccl. 12:13**

As we look at the Seventh-day Adventist Church today, we have every reason to take courage. Never in its history have we seen such an upsurge of ministries by Seventh-day Adventists that are independant of the church organisation. Never before have we seen the great truths contained in the books of the Spirit of Prophecy being printed and distributed at low cost by independant publishers. Many independant colporteurs, while selling low-cost copies of Desire of Ages, Bible Readings and Great Controversy are deluged with opportunities to explain the three angels' messages to enquiring souls—especially those who have questioned the dogmas of Roman Catholicism.

Independant ministries are not new. Wherever and whenever God's appointed agents have faltered, there have arisen messengers of God, ready and able to fill the gap. When Elder Daniells and others showed their determination to organise in a way contrary to the instruction of Mrs White, she began to encourage the setting up of self-supporting work. She actually helped to set up a self-supporting school near Madison, Tennisee, USA, and instructed the two principal founders, Brethren E.A. Sutherland, and Percy T. Magan, to stay separate from the organisation. (Refer Spalding-Magan Collection of E.G.W. Unpublished Testimonies, p.411, 412)*                    1.

Today, with the understandable proliferation
of independant ministries, Satan as ever, seeks
any opportunity to jump on the band waggon and
divert ministry from its rightful course.  We
should be aware that such ministries are particularly vulnerable through their Boards of Directors, which can be infiltrated relatively easily
by imposters in the same way as institutions and
sections of the organised body of the church
have been diverted from their original purposes.
It seems that the smaller the ministry and the
simpler its type of organisation, the less vulnerable it is to Satan's plans. This is why
there is no substitute for committed men and
women who, acting as individuals under the
unction of the Holy Spirit, develop their God-
given talents and allow themselves to be used of
God to save precious souls.

Nowhere is such ministry more apparent than
in lands where the Church has succumbed to the
demands of state and abandoned those of its
membership who refuse to bow to Baal. Today in
Hungary, the largest single congregation of
people claiming to follow the truth as revealed
to Seventh-day Adventists is to be found outside
of the General Conference and State-recognised
churches. The unrecognised congregations are
rapidly increasing because they have not abandoned the message as revealed to God's remnant
people following 1844.

Independent reports from Christian organisations concerned with religious affairs in the
USSR indicate that the "underground" branches of
Christianity are thriving.  In the case of those
calling themselves Seventh-day Adventists, it is
estimated that there are more in the "underground" church than in the officially-recognised

church.

Many sincere members of the Seventh-day Adventist church have come to regard the church as Babylon. This they suppose to be true as they see that Babylonians have taken over control of some key positions in our work. But to accept such a proposition is merely to legitimise the position of those usurpers who have set up a papal-like form of government to promote heresies of the anti-Christ. In modern parlance, it's like accepting the authority of hi-jackers.

Such imposters are not new to Adventism. Mrs White went to considerable pains to point out that the remnant church is not, and cannot be, Babylon. Such would be a contradiction in terms, for it is the remnant or last church which gives the call "to come out of Babylon, and to keep God's commandments". It has the testimony of Jesus. Such an assumption would be self-destroying and illogical. In 1893, Sister White was constrained to write to a 'Brother S' in Napier, New Zealand:

> My brother, if you are teaching that the Seventh-day Adventist church is Babylon, you are wrong. (<u>Testimonies to Ministers and Gospel Workers</u>, p.59)

She had just explained to 'Brother S' that:
> the second angel's message was to go to Babylon [the churches] proclaiming her downfall, and calling the people to come out of her. The same message is to be proclaimed the second time. 'And after these things I saw another angel come down from heaven, having great power, and the earth was lightened with His glory. And he cried mightily with a strong voice, saying Babylon the great is fallen, is fallen, and is become

the habitation of devils, and the hold of
every foul spirit, and a cage of every
unclean and hateful bird... And I heard
another voice from heaven, saying, Come out
of her My people, that ye be not partakers of
her sins and that ye receive not of her
plagues...' (Ibid p.59)

And so, loyal Seventh-day Adventists today,
are faced with a dilemma. They see the church
being controlled by some who, far from calling
people to come out of Babylon, are deliberately
mis-using the resources of the Church to take us
back to Babylon! Are we to stand idly by and
support such subversive activities by our
silence? As stewards of God, have we not been
given the responsibility to see that the means
entrusted to us are used fully to warn the world
of the great judgment-hour message?

Fortunately, God in His great wisdom and
mercy has not left His people without a prophet
to guide us through end-time events. We shall
turn to inspiration for guidance and re-
assurance.

Contrary to what some of our leaders may wish
us to believe, the General Conference does not
constitute God's remnant church as claimed in a
U.S. Supreme court (See chapter 25) Paul defines
the church of the living God as "the pillar and
ground of truth". (1 Tim. 3:15). Seventh-day
Adventists have traditionally believed that we
have been entrusted with the truth for the last
days of earth's history. Of this church, God's
messenger has said:

God has a church on earth who are lifting up
the downtrodden law, and presenting to the
world the Lamb of God that taketh away the
sins of the world. The church is the deposi-

tory of the wealth of the riches of the grace of Christ, and through the church eventually will be made manifest the final and full display of the love of God to the world that is to be lightened with its glory. (<u>Testimonies to Ministers</u>, p.50)

If the General Conference of SDAs circulates teaching contrary to the "pillars and ground of the truth", can it honestly claim to be the voice of God? Mrs White was constrained to pass judgment on our General Conference leaders back in the year 1901, for less obvious heresies:

That these men should stand in the sacred place to be the voice of God to the people, as we once believed the General Conference to be, that is past. (<u>G.C. Bulletin</u> 1901, p.25)

That is why God's Messenger called for, and got, a re-organisation of the General Conference. But as we have seen, this re-organisation was all too short-lived. How much more applicable are the words of the prophet for today:

A strange thing has come into our churches. Men who are placed in positions of responsibility that they may be wise helpers to their fellow workers have come to suppose that they were set as kings and rulers in the churches to say to one brother, do this; to another, do that; and to another, be sure to labour in such and such a way. (<u>Testimonies to Ministers</u> p.477)

Is not this the spirit which now motivates the actions of leaders who refuse to allow loyal Adventist veterans to travel around the conferences feeding the words of life to truth-starved souls? Are such so-called leaders able to transmit the will of God? According to Mrs White, we place in peril our own salvation when we sanction or assist those who are not in harmony with truth and righteousness:

I call upon God's people to open their eyes. When you sanction or carry out the decisions of men who, as you know, are not in harmony with truth and righteousness, you weaken your own faith, and lose your relish for communion with God. (Testimonies to Ministers p. 91)

As if this warning were not enough, God's servant warns of terrible woes against both those who carry on, and those who support the work of an unsanctified ministry:

If God pronounces a woe upon those who are called to preach the truth and refuse to obey, a heavier woe rests upon those who take upon them this sacred work without clean hands and pure hearts. As there are woes for those who preach the truth while they are unsanctified in heart and life, so there are woes for those who receive and 'maintain' the unsanctified in the position which they cannot fill. (2 Testimonies p. 552)

Does Mrs White have anything else to say about supporting those who are not upholding the messages entrusted to Seventh-day Adventists? Yes, she does:

It would be poor policy to support from the treasury of God those who really mar and injure His work, and who are constantly lowering the standard of Christianity. (3 Testimonies p. 553)

Do our leaders who have supported and continue to support such errors and/or fabrica-

tions as found in some of our official publications, come under the category of those who
mar and injure God's work? Hear the answer from
God's messenger:

> The men who close their eyes to divine light
> are ignorant, deplorably ignorant, both of
> the Scriptures and the power of God. The Holy
> Spirit's working is not agreeable to them,
> and they attribute its manifestations to
> fanaticism. They rebel against the light, and
> do all they can to shut it out, calling dark-
> ness light, and light darkness...
> Those who entertain and speak this belief do
> not know what they are talking about. They are
> cherishing a love of darkness; and just as
> long as these Christless souls are retained
> in positions of responsibility, the cause of
> God is imperilled. (Testimonies to Ministers
> p. 284)

So we see that as long as such leaders are in
position they are imperilling the cause of God!
(i.e. His church and its mission) These are the
ones who are exploiting the "new order" organization about which Mrs White warned. She gives
the reason why such men are attracted to presi-
dential types of government:

> But some men, as soon as they are placed in
> sacred positions of trust, regard themselves
> as great men; and this thought, if enter-
> tained, ends the desire for divine enlighten-
> ment, which is the only possible thing that
> can make men great. (Ibid)

Do we as stewards have a responsibility when
it comes to determining how we should support
God's work?  Or should we leave it up to the
"great men" to direct all the means which God

has entrusted to us? The Lord's anointed laid down a very important principle of stewardship when she sent special instruction from Cooranbong, New South Wales, relating to the Review and Herald office and work in Battle Creek:

> But the Lord has made us individually His stewards. We each hold a solemn responsibility to invest this means ourselves. God does not lay upon you the burden of asking the Conference, or any council of men, whether you shall use your means as you see fit to advance the work of God in destitute towns and cities and impoverished localities. (Letter No. 68, 1896)

As for the ultimate destination and purpose of the tithe, she was very definite:

> The tithe should go to those who labour in word and doctrine, be they men or women. (Evangelism, p.492)

Now, as Seventh-day Adventists, we know what kind of doctrinal preaching Mrs White is referring to, don't we?

Is it the kind of doctrine that robs Jesus Christ of His qualification to be our High Priest, by saying that He did not overcome while being tempted like us? (See Heb 4:15)

Is it the kind of doctrine that tells us that Christ's atonement was completed at the cross and thus gives support to the popular Evangelical view that His work of salvation was also complete, and there is therefore no need for an investigative judgment?

Is it the kind of doctrine that appears to Adventists to uphold still the historic belief in the judgment, yet seeks to maintain some credibility with the Evangelicals by putting God in the "hot seat" and judging Him?

The answer, of course, is perfectly obvious. Such preachers are the ones that have got our church organisation into bed with the popular evangelicals – the daughters of Babylon! They are not the people whom Mrs White describes as being worthy of the tithe because they do not "labour in word and doctrine". **They labour with "cunning" words and "craftiness" as described by Paul, to undermine our doctrines!** (Eph. 4:14)

These are the leaders who, because they are the equivalent of biblical hirelings, will desert the cause of God. They will not stay in the church once they are deprived of their sustenance and experience persecution. Such a time is known as the "Shaking Time" and this shaking experience has already started in the Seventh-day Adventist church especially in lands where there is state and church intolerance of religion. Back in 1876, Mrs White said:

> God is now sifting His people—testing their purposes and their motives. Many will be but as chaff—no wheat, no value in them. (4 Testimonies p.51)

And in 1900 she warned about failure to obey what God has set before us as truth:

> We are in the shaking time, the time when everything that can be shaken will be shaken. The Lord will not excuse those who know the truth if they do not in word and deed obey His commandments. (6 Testimonies p.332)

God in His mercy has extended the time of probation in our fair lands of Australasia. But His servant warns us:

> Just as soon as God's people are sealed and prepared for the shaking, it will come. In-

deed, it has begun already; the judgments of God are now upon the land, to give us warning, that we may know what is coming.(4 SDA Bible Commentary p.1161)

But God's followers must not be complacent, nor expect sanctification without obedience:

As the storm approaches, a large class who have professed faith in the third angel's message, but who have not been sanctified through obedience to the truth, abandon their position, and join the ranks of the opposition.(Great Controversy p.608)

Now is the time for every loyal follower of Christ, every committed Seventh-day Adventist, to encourage our fellow believers and warn those who have not as yet seen the light. To fail to do so is to sanction apostasy and invite spiritual disaster:

When you sanction or carry out the decisions of men who, as you know, are not in harmony with truth and righteousness, you weaken your own faith, and lose your relish for communion with God.(Testimonies to Ministers p.91)

Here is a warning and a promise:

The work which the church has failed to do in a time of peace and prosperity she will have to do in a terrible crisis under most discouraging circumstances... At that time the superficial, conservative class, whose influence has steadily retarded the progress of the work will renounce their faith. (5 Testimonies p. 463)

So, as we of God's remnant people, give the trumpet a "certain sound" we may take courage in the fact that those who are responsible for hindering the finishing of the work, and thus delaying Christ's return, will be removed from us. And again, the servant of the Lord says:

> In the absence of persecution there have drifted into our ranks, men who appear sound and their Christianity unquestionable, but who, if persecution should arise, would go out from us. (<u>Evangelism</u> p. 360)

In the light of increased willingness shown in recent years for certain leaders of our church to assiduously promote heresy under the cloak of supposed truth, how much more relevant are the warnings of our prophet to these closing days of earth's history! Only as we understand the sinister workings of the dragon's wrath against God's remnant people, can we interpret the signs in a way which will quell discouragement and enable us to fortify our minds and hearts for the great battle ahead. We will then be fully aware that:

> **The contest is between the commandments of God and the commandments of men. In this time, the gold will be separated from the dross in the church.**(<u>5 Testimonies</u> p.81)

If, through faith, we will follow Christ in His great saving work of atonement, it follows that we will have a faith that also enables obedience. God's power will then energise even those of us who are retiring and reticent by nature:

> Those who have been timid and self-distrustful, will declare themselves openly for Christ and His truth. The most weak and hesitating in the church, will be as David - willing to do and dare. (Ibid)

The final stages of the Church's march to victory will not be characterised by timidity, doubts and despair.  Memories of those who have led God's children into apostasy will, with their heresies, be reduced to mere asterisks in the great controversy between Christ and Satan. God's prophet has dramatically portrayed the remnant church of Christ when it has been purged of "dross" as a pure but militant army:

> fair as the moon, clear as the sun, terrible as an army with banners. (5 Testimonies p.82)

God's messenger to the remnant is not describing an army of people who have been tricked into following the commandments of men. No!  She is speaking of those who keep the commandments of God and proclaim the message of 1844 to Evermore.

*1.Madison college was later absorbed into the organised work and eventually ceased to exist.

# APPENDICES

**Evangelist J.B. Conley on Nature of Christ**
Australian Signs of the Times, 25 May 1948

...But the Scriptures have placed the identity of antichrist beyond either guesswork or confusion. The Bible has clearly named the guilty one. John says that he denies that "Jesus Christ is come in the flesh." 2 John 7. Let this be the first mark of antichrist by which his identity will be placed beyond dispute. The verse does not say that antichrist denies that Jesus is come, but that he denies "He is come in the flesh." Far from denying the existence of Christ, the text suggests that antichrist teaches that Christ has come but teaches a doctrine about His coming which denies that "He is come in the flesh." If the Catholic Church is guilty, as the Protestant Reformers claimed her to be, then her teaching concerning the nature of Jesus in His incarnation into this world as a babe will reveal it. Let us examine that teaching in the light of the text before us.

The Bible teaches that Jesus was born into the world through Mary, who was a direct descendent of Adam. By inheritance she partook of Adam's nature. Adam's nature was mortal and subject to death as a result of the transgression of God's will in Eden. His flesh was by nature that of the "children of wrath". Mary partook of this nature in all its aspects. She was a representative of the whole human race, and in no way different from others descended from Adam's line. She was "favoured among women" only because she was the one chosen of God through whom the "mystery of godliness was to be made manifest", and through whom Jesus was to be incarnated into the fleshly state of Adam's race. It was God's purpose that through a divine miracle Jesus should be brought from heaven, where He had been one with the Father in the Godhead, to be born into the human family, there to partake of all the temptations to which Adam's race is subject. This was possible only as He would partake of the nature of Adam's race. Of this Paul says, "Forasmuch then as the children are partakers of flesh and blood, He also Himself likewise took part of the same... Wherefore in all things it behoved Him to be made like unto His brethren." Heb. 2:14-17.

If further evidence were needed the same writer supplied it. In 1 Tim.3:16 he records: "Great is the mystery of godliness. God was manifest in the flesh." Here, he says, is the mystery of godliness, the ability of Jesus to come from heaven, suffer Himself to be manifest in human flesh, and yet to live sinlessly.

This latter fact antichrist was to deny. He was to deny that Jesus came in a divine manifestation which brought Him in all phases of His nature to partake of the weakness of Adam's race. He would deny that Jesus came "in the flesh," the same flesh as that of mortal men. On this first count, the denial that Jesus "is come in the flesh," the Catholic Church stands convicted of guilt and thus is identified by the marks of antichrist. Through the teaching of the "Immaculate Conception of Mary," that she was preserved from all original sin, they in theory provide "different flesh" from that of the rest of Adam's race to be the avenue through which Jesus was incarnated into the plan of salvation. To state their teaching with authority, it will be best to quote our evidence from Catholic authors.

Our first proof will be from the pen of Cardinal Gibbons in his book, "Faith of Our Fathers," pages 203,204. He says: "We define that the blessed Virgin Mary in the first moment of her conception... was preserved free from the taint of original sin. Unlike the rest of the children of Adam, the soul of Mary was never subject to sin."

Cardinal Gibbons has here clearly stated the teaching of the Roman Catholic Church concerning the sinlessness of the Virgin Mary. It is a teaching not taught in the Bible, but which has been introduced by Catholic teachers who claim to have authority even above that of the Scriptures, in matters of doctrine.

Here I would ask my readers, both Protestant and Catholic, to ponder carefully what this teaching does to the gospel plan. It means that if Mary was born without sin and was preserved from sin for the express purpose of bringing Jesus into the world, then Jesus was born of holy flesh, which was different from that of the rest of Adam's race. This means that He did not take upon Himself our kind of flesh and blood, and in His incarnation did not identify Himself with humanity. It means, too, that He was not tempted "in all points" as we were. It means that Paul was all wrong when he wrote the Book of Hebrews in which he declares that Jesus "also Himself likewise took part of the same" flesh as the rest of Adam's race, that "in all things" He was made "like unto His brethren" Heb. 2:14,17. But above all this, if the Catholic teaching is true, then Jesus, not having come within reach of humanity by partaking of man's nature, cannot be the "one mediator between God and men." Nor can we "come boldly unto the throne of grace that we may obtain mercy, and find grace to help in time of need" Heb. 4:16. All this plays conveniently into the hands of the Catholic plan of salvation. It opens wide the door for the intercession of the Virgin Mary and the respective "saints", who form part of the papal mediatorial system. And moreover, it places in the hands of the priesthood the power to usurp authority which God in the Scriptures has never delegated to them - that of being controllers of the approaches to the throne of mercy.

At this stage of our review of the subject of antichrist, I believe all fairminded people will acknowledge that if the Papacy is not the antichrist it has been singularly unfortunate in being so like the scriptural description of him. In the papal claim that Jesus was born of one who had been "preserved from every taint of original sin" and who "unlike the rest of the children of Adam ...was never subject to sin," we find the first mark of antichrist indelibly implanted. The Papacy certainly teaches that Jesus Christ did "not come in the flesh".

**Elder A.T. Jones' letter to G.C. President A.G. Daniells** Jan.26,1906 (Portions Only)

Then came the General Conference at Battle Creek. According to the arrangements I was to report the proceedings of the Conference; and according to the arrangements, Brothers Prescott and Waggoner were not expected evidently to have even that much to do. But before the Conference actually assembled in session, there occurred that meeting in the Library room of the College Building, in which Sister White spoke on General Conference matters and organization, declaring that there must be "an entire new organization and to have a Committee that shall take in not merely half a dozen that is to be a ruling and controlling power, but it is to have representatives of those that are placed in responsibility in our educational interests in our Sanitariums, etc., that there should be a renovation without delay. To have this Conference pass on and close up as the Conferences have done, with the same manipulating with the very same tone, and the same order - God forbid! God forbid brethren... And until this come we might just as well close up the Conference today as any other day... This thing has been continued for the last fifteen years or more, (1901 minus 15 takes us back to 1886), and God calls for a change.

"God wants a change, and it is high time - it is high time that there was ability that should connect with the Conference, with the General Conference right here in this city. Not wait until it is done and over with, and then gather up the forces and see what can be done. We want to know what can be done right now. "From the light that I have, as it was presented to me in figures. There was a narrow compass here; there within that narrow compass is a king-like, a kingly ruling power. God means what He says and He says, "I want a change here." "Will it be the same thing? Going over and over the same ideas, the same committees - and here is the little throne - the king is in there, and these others are all secondary. God wants those committees that have been handling things for so long should be relieved of their command and have a chance for their life and see if they cannot get out of this rut that they are in - which I have no hope of their getting out of, because the Spirit of God has been working and working, and yet the king is in there still. Now the Lord wants His Spirit to come in. He wants the Holy Ghost King.

"From the light that I have had for some time, and has been expressed, over and over again, not to all that are here, but has been expressed to individuals - the plan, that God would have all to work from, that never should one mind or two minds or three minds, nor four minds, or a few minds I should say be considered of sufficient wisdom and power to control and mark out plans and let it rest upon the minds of one or two or three in regard to this broad field that we have.

"And the work all over our field demands an entirely different course of action than we have had; that there needs the laying of a found- ation that is different from what we have had... In all these countries, far, and near, He wants to be an arousing, broadening, enlarging power. And a management which is getting confused in itself - not that anyone is wrong or means to be wrong, but the principle is wrong, and the principles have become so mixed and so fallen from what God's principles are.

213

"These things have been told, and this standstill has got to come to an end. But yet every
Conference has woven after the same pattern,
it is the very same loom that carries it, and
finally it will come to nought."

She declared that God wants us to take hold
of this work, every human agency. Each one is
to act in their capacity in such a way that
the confidence of the whole people will be established in them and that they will not be afraid,
but see everything just as light as day until
they are in connection with the work of God
and the whole people... All the provision was
made in heaven, all the facilities, all the
riches of the grace of God was imparted to every
worker that was connected with the cause, and
every one of these are wholly dependent upon
God. And when we leave God out of the question,
and allow hereditary and cultivated traits of
character to come in, let me tell you, we are
on very slippery ground.

God hath His servants - His Church, established
in the earth, composed of many members, but
of one body; that in every part of the work
one part must work as connected with another
part, and that with another part, and with another
part, and these are joined together by the golden
links of heaven and there is to be no kings
in the midst of all. There is to be no man that
has the right to put his hand out and say:
No you can not go there. We won't support you if
you go there. Why, what have you to do with the
supporting? Did you create the means? The means
comes from the people. And those who are in
destitute fields - the voice of God has told
me to instruct them to go to the people and
tell them their necessities, and to draw all
the people to work just where they can find

a place to work, to build up the work in every place they can.

Upon that instruction and much more to the same effect in that talk you and Brother Prescott and others took hold of the matter pertaining to the then pending General Conference (1901), set aside entirely the old order of things, and started it new. At the opening of the General Conference, April 2, Sister White spoke briefly to the same effect as in the College Building the day before. Brother Irwin followed with a few words; and then you spoke a few words and introduced a motion that the usual rules and precedents for arranging and transacting the business of the Conference be suspended, and the General Committee be hereby appointed... to constitute a general or central committee, which shall do such work as necessarily must be done in providing the work of the Conference, and preparing the business to bring before the delegates. Thus the new order of things was started.

The night of that very first day of the conference, I was appointed to preach the sermon. Since I had been appointed to report the proceedings I expected to have no preaching or other work to do. Therefore when I was called to preach, I supposed that it was designed to have me preach that one time during the conference, and have me do it at the beginning, so that I could go on afterwards unmolested with the reporting. I spoke on Church Organization. When that meeting was over, I supposed that my preaching during the Conference was done. Therefore, I was surprised when only two days afterwards - April 4, you came to me at the reporter's table and said we want you to preach to-night! I said I supposed that my preaching was over, since I have the

reporting to do. I can not do this and preach
often. You said to me, "You have light for the
people, and we want them to have it." I consented
and preached again on the subject of Church
Organization, developing the subject further,
and on the same principles precisely as on the
night of April 2.

In that Conference (1901) the General Conference
was started toward the called-for-reorganization.
All understood that the call was away from
a centralized order of things in which one man
or two men or three or four men or a few men
held the ruling and directing power, to an organization in which, all the people as individuals
should have a part, with God, in Christ, by
the Holy Spirit as the unifying, and directing
power. Indeed, the day before my second sermon
on organization, Sister White had said, April
3, we want to understand that there are no gods
in our Conference. There are to be no kings
here, and no kings in any Conference that is
formed, "All ye are brethren."

"The Lord wants to bind those at this Conference
heart to heart. No man is to say I am a god,
and you must do as I say. From the beginning
to the end this is wrong. There is to be an
individual work. God says, "Let him take hold
of My strength that he may make peace with Me
and he shall make peace with Me."

"Remember that God can give wisdom to those
who handle His work. It is not necessary to
send thousands of miles to Battle Creek for
advice, and then have to wait weeks before an
answer can be received. Those who are right
on the ground are to decide what shall be done.
You know what you have to wrestle with, but
those who are thousands of miles away do not
know." Bulletin 1901, pp.69,70. And on the very

day of my second sermon, April 4, she said in a talk at 9.00 a.m., this meeting will determine the character of our work in the future. How important that every step shall be taken under the supervision of God. This work must be carried in a very different manner to what it has been in the past years - Bulletin 1901, p.83.

In this understanding an entire new Constitution was adopted; and that such was the understanding in adopting this Constitution is plainly shown in the discussions. Under this Constitution the General Conference Committee was composed of a large number of men, with power to organize itself by choosing a chairman etc. No president of the General Conference was chosen; nor was provided for. The presidency of the General Conference was eliminated to escape a centralized power, a one-man power, a king-ship, a monarchy. The Constitution was framed and adopted to that end in accordance with the whole guiding thought in the Conference from the beginning in that room in the College Building.

Shortly after the Conference ended, you suggested during the meeting at Indianapolis that my sermon on organization ought to be printed in a leaflet so that our people everywhere could have it for study in the work of reorganization. Your suggestion was agreed to and I was directed to prepare it for printing. I did so and it was printed at General Conference direction in Words of Truth Series No. 31, Extra May 1901.

Now after all this, it was not long before the whole spirit and principle of General Conference Organization and affairs began to be reversed again. This spirit of reaction became so rife and so rank that some before the General Conference of 1903 at Oakland, Calif., two men, or three men, or four men, or a few men I should say, being together in Battle Creek of somewhere else, and without any kind of authority, but directly against the plain words of the Constitution, took it absolutely upon themselves to elect you president, and Brother Prescott vice-president of the General Conference. And than that there never was in this universe a clearer piece of usurpation of position, power and authority. You two were then of right, just as much president and vice-president of Timbuktu as you were of the Seventh-day Adventist General Conference.

But this spirit did not stop even there. The thing was done directly against the Constitution. This was too plain to be escaped. And it was just as plain that with that Constitution still perpetuated in the coming General Conference, this usurpation of position, power, and authority could not be perpetuated. What could be done to preserve the usurpation - Oh, that was just as easy as the other. A new Constitution was framed to fit and to uphold the usurpation. This Constitution was carried to the General Conference of 1903 at Oakland, Calif., and in every unconstitutional way, because in every truly constitutional government the constitution comes in some way from the people, not from the monarch. Thus the people make and establish a Constitution. The monarch grants a Constitution. When the people make a Constitution the people govern. When a monarch grants a Constitution, he seeks to please the people with a toy and keeps the government himself. This difference is the sole difficulty in Russia to-day; and the difference is simply the difference between monarchy and government of the people; and between oppression and freedom. The people want to make a Constitution. The Czar wants to grant them a constitution, and have them endorse anew his autocracy and bureaucracy by adopting the Constitution that he grants.

And this is just the difference between the General Conference and its Constitution of 1901 and the General Conference and its Constitution of 1903. In 1901 the monarchy was swept aside completely, and the Conference itself as such and as a whole made a new Constitution. In the General Conference of 1903 the usurpers of monarchial position and authority came with the Constitution that fitted and maintained their usurpation, and succeeded in getting it adopted. And how? - None of the people had asked for a new Constitution. The General Conference delegation had asked for it. Not even the Committee on Constitution asked for it. In behalf of the usurpation it was brought before that Committee and advocated there, because, in very words, "The Church must have a visible head". It was not even then nor was it ever, favoured by that Committee. It was put through the Committee, and reported to the Conference, only by permanently dividing the Committee, - a minority, of the Committee, opposing it all the time, and - a thing almost unheard of in Seventh-day Adventist Conferences, a minority report against it. And when at last it was adopted by the final vote, it was by a slim majority of just five. And it was only by the carelessness of some of the delegates that it got through even that way; for there were just then downstairs in the Oakland Church enough delegates who were opposed to it, to have defeated it if they had been present. They told this themselves afterwards. But they did not know that the vote was being taken, and by their not being in their places, the usurpation was sanctioned; the re-

actionary spirit that had been so long working
for absolute control had got it; the principles
and intent of the General Conference of 1901
was reversed; and a Czardom was enthroned which
has since gone steadily onward in the same way
and has with perfect consistency built up a
thorough bureaucratic government, by which it
reaches and meddles with, and manipulates, the
affairs of all, not only of the union and local
conferences, but of local churches, and of individual persons. So that some of the oldest men
in active service to-day, and who by their life
experiences are best qualified to know, have
freely said that in the whole history of the
denomination there has never been such a one-
man power, such a centralized despotism, so
much of Papacy, as there has been since the
Oakland Conference (of 1903). And as a part
of this bureaucracy there is, of all the incongruous things ever heard of, a Religious Liberty
Bureau - a contradiction in terms.

Now when I was opposed to this thing before
and in the General Conference of 1897, and before
and in the General Conference of 1899, and before
and in the General Conference of 1901, and before
and in the General Conference of 1903, why should
you be perplexed that I have not fallen in with
it and helped to make it a success since 1903?
Why should I in 1903, abandon all the principles
and teachings by which I was right in opposing
it, until and including 1903, when I was in
the right all these years in opposing it and
doing all that I could to keep it from succeeding,
why and upon what principles should I have swung
in and favoured it just because at last in a
most arbitrary, unconstitutional and usurping
way it did at last succeed?

Again in the General Conference of 1901 you

yourself said that in the principles of organization that I preached I had "light for the
people". Those principles were the ones that
prevailed in that Conference; and at your own
suggestion these principles as preached in my
first sermon, were published for the help of
the denomination in the work of reorganization.
But the principles and the form of organization
of 1903 were directly the opposite of those
that in 1901 you said were "light for the people".
If my second sermon in the General Conference
of 1901 had been printed along with the first,
the people would have been able to see more
plainly how entirely the course of things in
1903 was the reverse of that in 1901. And anyone
can see it now by reading The General Conference
Bulletin of 1901, pp.37-42, and pp.101-105.
 Now brother, were those principles light in
1901? If so, then what did you do when you exposed
the opposite of them in 1902, 1903? Or were
those principles light in 1901, and darkness
in 1903? Or were those principles really darkness
in 1901 when you said that they were light.
Or are they still light today as they were in
1901? And if in the General Conference of 1901
you were not able to distinguish between light
and darkness what surety has anybody that you
were any more able to do it in 1902-1903? Or
is it possible that in 1902-1903 you were not,
and now are not, able to see that the principles
and the course of action of 1902-1903 are not
the same as those of the General Conference
of 1901? In other words, is it possible that
you can think that certain principles with their
course of action, and the reverse of them are
one and the same? I know that the principles
that in 1901 you said were "light for the people"
were then really light, and that they are now

light and forever more will be light. They are only plain principles of the Word of God. I hold these principles today exactly as I did in 1901 and long before, and shall hold them forever. For this cause I was opposed to the usurpation and unconstitutional action of 1902-1903 that were the opposite of these principles; and shall always be opposed to them.

In view of all these facts again I ask, Why should you think that I should abandon all, just because you and some others did? I think that it was enough for me to keep still these three years. It is true that I have had no disposition to do anything but keep still about it. For when the General Conference of 1903 made their choice that way, I have no obligation to their having what they have chosen. I have no disposition to oppose it in any other way than by preaching the gospel. Indeed the strongest possible opposition that can be made to it is the plain, simple preaching of the plain gospel. There is this about it, however, that now the plain simple preaching of the plain gospel will be considered disloyal to the General Conference, disloyal to the organization, etc. Nevertheless, I am going to continue to preach the plain gospel, and that gospel is in the Word of God. For when the General Conference and the organized work put themselves in such a position that the plain preaching of the gospel as in the Word of God is disloyalty to the General Conference and the "organized work", then the thing to do is to preach the gospel, as it is in the Word of God...

In 1901 the General Conference was turned away from a centralized power; a one man or two men, or three men, or four men, or a few men power, a kingship, a monarchy; because the instructions was in very words, the principle is wrong. It will not do to say that in 1902-1903 circumstances had changed. For whatever change may even occur in circumstances, principles never change.

I stated that the present order of General Conference affairs is a thoroughly bureaucratic government. Not every section of it is called a bureau; but that is what in practice every section is, whatever it may be called; and the title of the Religious Liberty Bureau is expressive of the whole.

I stated that the phrase "Religious Liberty Bureau" is a contradiction in terms, on every principle that is the truth. There are many words of our language that are the result and expression of invariable human experience through ages.

The result of human experience through ages has in certain things been so invariable that a word tells it, and tells it so truly, when that word is used, that a certain order of things is described; and when that word is espoused, then we have in certainty the situation and order of things which the word expresses. Bureaucracy - Government by bureaus - is one of these words: and the definition, which is but the expression of ages of invariable experience is as follows:-

"Bureaucracy: Government by bureaus: specifically, excessive multiplication of, and concentration of power in, administrative bureaus. The principle of bureaucracy tends to official interference in many of the properly private affairs of life, and to the inefficient and obtrusive performance of duty through minute subdivisions of functions, inflexible formality, and pride of place". - Century Dictionary.

"A bureaucracy is sure to think that its duty

is to augment official power, official business,
or official numbers, rather than to leave free
the energies of mankind." – Standard Dictionary.

### M.L. Andreasen on 'The Atonement'
"Letters to the Churches," No. 6, 1959

The serious student of the atonement is likely to be perplexed when he consults the Spirit of Prophecy to find two sets of apparently contradictory statements in regard to the atonement. He will find that when Christ "offered Himself on the cross, a perfect atonement was made for the sins of the people." Signs of the Times, June 28, 1899. He will find that the Father bowed before the cross "in recognition of its perfection. 'It is enough' He said, 'the atonement is complete'"Review & Herald, September 24, 1901.

But in Great Controversy he will find this: "At the conclusion of the 2300 days, in 1844, Christ entered the Most Holy place of the heavenly sanctuary, to perform the closing work of the atonement" page 422. In Patriarchs & Prophets, 357, I read that sins will "stand on record in the sanctuary until the final atonement." (in 1844) Page 358 states that in "the final atonement the sins of the truly penitent are to be blotted from the records of heaven." Early Writings, 253 says that "Jesus entered the Most Holy of the heavenly at the end of the 2300 days of Daniel 8, to make the final atonement."

The first set of statements says that the atonement was made on the cross; the other says that the final atonement was made 1800 years later. I have found seven statements that the atonement was made on the cross; I have twenty-two statements that the final atonement was made in heaven. Both of these figures are doubtless incomplete; for there may be others that have escaped my attention. It is evident, however that I may not accept one set of statements and reject the other if I wish to arrive at truth. The question therefore is which statements are true? Which are false? or, are both true? If so, how can they be harmonized?

I was perplexed when in the February issue of the Ministry 1957, I found the statement that "the sacrificial act of the cross (was) a complete, perfect, and final atonement." This was in distinct contradiction to Mrs White's pronouncement that the final atonement began in 1844. I thought that this might be a misprint, and wrote to Washington calling attention to the matter, but found it was not a misprint but an official and approved statement. If we still hold the Spirit of Prophecy as of authority we therefore have two contradictory beliefs: the final atonement was made at the cross; the final atonement began in 1844.

I have listened to several discussions of the meaning of the Hebrew word "kaphar" which is the word used in the original for atonement, but have received little help. The best definition I have found is a short explanatory phrase in Patriarchs & Prophets, 358, which simply states that the atonement "the great work of Christ, or blotting out of sin, was represented by the services on the day of atonement."

This definition is in harmony with Lev.16:30 which says that "the priest shall make an atonement for you, to cleanse you, that ye may be clean from all your sins before the Lord." Atonement is here equated with being "clean from all your sins." As sin was the cause of separation between God and man, the removing of sin would again unite God and man. And this would be at-one-ment.

Christ did not need any atonement, for He and the Father were always one John 10:30. Christ prayed for His disciples "that they may all be one, as Thou, Father, art in Me and I in

226

Thee, that they may be one in Us." John 17:21.

The definition of atonement as consisting of three words at-one-ment is by some considered obsolete, but it nevertheless represents vital truth. Mrs White thus uses it. Says she: "unless they accept the atonement provided for them in the remedial sacrifice of Jesus Christ who is our atonement, at-one-ment with God" Manuscript 122, 1901.

God's plan is that in "the fullness of time He might gather together in one all things in Christ." Eph.1:10. When this is done, "the family of heaven and the family of earth are one." "Desire of Ages" 835. Then "one pulse of harmony and gladness beats through the vast creation." "Great Controversy" 678. At last the atonement is complete.

## Two Phases of the Atonement

Much confusion in regard to the Atonement arises from a neglect to recognize the two divisions of the atonement. Note what is said of John the Baptist, "He did not distinguish clearly the two phases of Christ's work - as a suffering sacrifice, and a conquering king" "Desire of Ages" 136,137. The book "Questions On Doctrine" makes the same mistake. It does not distinguish clearly; in fact it does not distinguish at all; it does not seem to know of the two phases; hence the confusion.

## The First Phase

The first phase of Christ's atonement was that of a suffering sacrifice. This began before the world was, included the incarnation, Christ's life on earth, the temptation in the wilderness, Gethsemane, Golgotha, and ended when God's voice called Christ from the "stony prison house of death". The fifty third chapter of Isaiah is a vivid picture of this.

Satan had overcome Adam in the garden of Eden, and in a short time nearly the whole world had come under his sway. At the time of Noah there were only eight souls who entered the ark. Satan claimed to be prince of this world, and no one had challenged him.

But God did not recognize Satan's claim to dominion, and when Christ came to earth, the Father "gave the world into the hands of the Son, that through His mediatorial work He may completely vindicate the holiness and the binding claims of every precept of the divine law" Bible Echo, January 1887. This was a challenge to Satan's claim, and thus began in earnest the great controversy between Christ and Satan.

"Christ took the place of fallen Adam. With the sins of the world laid upon Him, He would go over the ground where Adam stumbled" Review & Herald February 24, 1874. "Jesus volunteered to meet the highest claims of the law" Ibid., September 2, 1890. "Christ made Himself responsible for every man and woman on earth" Ibid., February 27, 1900.

As Satan claimed ownership of the earth, it was necessary for Christ to overcome Satan before He could take possession of His kingdom. Satan knew this, and hence made an attempt to kill Christ as soon as He was born. However, as a contest between Satan and a helpless child in a manger, would not be fair, God frustrated this.

The first real encounter between Christ and Satan took place in the wilderness. After forty days of fasting Christ was weak and emaciated, at death's door. At this time Satan made his attack. But Christ resisted, even "unto blood" and Satan was compelled to retire defeated. But he did not give up. Throughout Christ's ministry, Satan dogged His footsteps, and made every moment a hard battle.

### Gethsemane

The climax of Christ's struggle with Satan, came in the garden of Gethsemane. Hitherto Christ had been upheld by the knowledge of the approval of the Father. But now He "was overpowered by the terrible fear that God was removing His presence from Him" "Spirit of Prophecy" Vol.3,p.95. If God should forsake Him, could He still resist Satan and die rather than yield? "Three times His humanity shrank from the last crowning sacrifice... The fate of humanity trembled in the balance" Ibid. 99. "As the Father's presence was withdrawn, they saw Him sorrowful with a bitterness or sorrow exceeding that of the last struggle with death" "Desire of Ages" 759. "He fell dying to the ground" but with His last ounce of strength murmured "If this cup may not pass from me except I drink it, Thy will be done... "A heavenly peace rested upon His bloodstained face. He had borne that which no human being could ever bear; He had tasted the sufferings of death for every man" "Desire of Ages" 694. In His death, He was victor.

"When Christ said 'It is finished' God responded 'It is finished, the human race shall have another trial'. The redemption price is paid, and Satan fell like lightning from heaven" Manuscript 11, 1897.

"As the Father beheld the cross He was satisfied. He said, 'It is enough, the offering is complete' Signs of the Times Sept. 30, 1899. It was necessary however, that there should be given the world a stern manifestation of the wrath of God, and so "in the grave Christ was the captive of divine justice" M.V.F. Feb. 24 1898. It must be abundantly attested that Christ's death was real, so He must "remain in the grave the allotted period of time" Review & Herald Apr. 26, 1898. When the time was expired a messenger was sent to relieve the Son of God from the debt for which He had become responsible, and for which He had made full atonement" Ms. 94, 1897.

"In the intercessory prayer of Jesus with His Father, He claimed that He had fulfilled the conditions which made it obligatory upon the Father to fulfill His part of the contract made in heaven with regard to fallen man. He prayed 'I have finished the work which Thou gavest Me to do' Mrs White makes this explanation, "That is, He had wrought out a righteous character on earth as an example for men to follow" "Spirit of Prophecy" Vol.3, 260.

The "contract" between the Father and the Son made in heaven, included the following:

1.  The Son was to work out a righteous character on earth as an example for man to follow."
2.  Not only was Christ to work out such a character, but He was to demonstrate that man also could do this; and thus man would become "more precious than fine gold, even a man than the golden wedge of Ophir."
3.  If Christ thus could present man as a new creature in Christ Jesus, then God was to "receive repentant and obedient men, and would love them even as He loves His Son" "Spirit of Prophecy" Vol.3,260; "Desire of Ages", 790.

Christ had fulfilled one phase of His priesthood by dying on the cross. He is now fulfilling another phase by pleading before the Father the case of repenting, believing sinners, presenting to God the offerings of His people" Ms. 42, 1901. "In His incarnation He had reached the prescribed limit as a sacrifice, but not as a redeemer" Ms. 11, 1897. On Golgotha He was the victim, the sacrifice. That was as far as He could go as a sacrifice. But now His work as a redeemer began. "When Christ cried 'It is finished' God's unseen hand rent the strong fabric which composed the veil of the temple from top to bottom. The way into the holiest of all was made manifest" Ibid.

With the cross the first phase of Christ's work as the "suffering sacrifice" ended. He had gone the "prescribed limit" as a sacrifice. He had finished His work "thus far." And now, with the Father's approval of the sacrifice, He was empowered to be the Saviour of mankind. At the ensuing coronation forty days later He was given all power in heaven and earth, and officially installed as High Priest.

### The Second Phase

"After His ascension our Saviour began His work as High Priest... In harmony with the typical service He began His ministration in the holy place, and at the termination of the prophetic days in 1844...He entered the most holy to perform the last division of His solemn work, to cleanse the sanctuary" Spirit of Prophecy" Vol.4, 265,266. On the same page, 266, Sister White repeats, apparently for emphasis, "at the termination of the 2300 days in 1844, Christ then entered the most holy place of the heavenly sanctuary, into the presence of God, to perform the closing work of atonement preparatory to His coming." The reader cannot fail to note how clearly and emphatically this is stated. John the Baptist "did not distinguish clearly the two phases of Christ's work, as a suffering

sacrifice and a conquering king" "Desire of Ages"
136,137. Our theologians are making the same
mistake today and are inexcusable. They have
light which John did not have.

In studying this part of the atonement, we
are entering a field that is distinctly Adventist,
and in which we differ from all other denominations.
This is our unique contribution to religion and theology, that which "has made us a separate people, and
has given character and power to our work." Counsels
to Editors & Writers, 54. In the same place she warns
us against making "void the truths of the atonement,
and destroy our confidence in the doctrines which
we have held sacred since the third angel's message
was first given.

This is vital counsel, and written for this
very time when efforts are being made by some
among us to have others believe that we are
like the churches about us, an evangelical body
and not a sect. Paul, in his day, had the same
heresy to meet. He was accused of being a "pest-
ilent fellow" a "ringleader of the sect of the
Nazarenes" Acts 24:5. In his answer before Felix
Paul confessed that after the "way which they
call a sect, so serve I the God of our Fathers
believing all things which are according to
the law and which are written in the prophets"
Act 24:14 R.V. In those days men spoke sneeringly
of the true church as a sect, as men do now.
Paul was not disturbed by this. We have no record
that he attempted to have the church of the
living God recognized as an evangelical body
by men who trampled the law of God in the dust.
On the contrary, whatever they might call him
and his "sect" he confessed that he believed
"all things which are written in the law and
the prophets" Verse 14.

The religious journal, "Christianity Today",

states in the March 3, 1958 issue, that "the Adventists today are contending vigorously that they are truly evangelical. They appear to want to be so regarded." Mentioning the book "Questions On Doctrine", it says that this "is the Adventist answer to the question whether it ought to be thought of as a sect or a fellow evangelical denomination." It states further that "the book" is published in an effort to convince the religious world that we are evangelical and one of them.

This is a most interesting and dangerous situation. As one official who was not in favour of what was being done stated to me: "We are being sold down the river." What a sight for heaven and earth! The church of the living God which has been given the commission to preach the gospel to every creature under heaven and call men to come out of Babylon, is now standing at the door of these churches asking permission to enter and become one of them. How are the mighty fallen! Had their plan succeeded, we might now be a member of some evangelical association and not a distinctive Seventh-day Adventist church any more, in secrecy "sold down the river." This is more than apostasy. This is giving up Adventism. It is the rape of a whole people. It is denying God's leading in the past. It is the fulfilment of what the Spirit of Prophecy said some years ago:

"The enemy of souls has sought to bring in the supposition that a great reformation was to take place among Seventh-day Adventists, and that this reformation would consist in giving up the doctrines which stand as pillars of our faith, and engaging in a process of reorganization. Were this reformation to take place, what would result? The principles of truth that God in His wisdom has given to the remnant church would be discarded. Our religion would be changed. "The fundamental principles that have sustained the work for the last fifty years would be accounted an error. A new organization would be established. Books of a new order would be written. A system of intellectual philosophy would be introduced... Nothing would be allowed to stand in the way of the new movement". Series B, No. 2, page 54,55.

"Be not deceived; many will depart from the faith, giving heed to seducing spirits and doctrines of devils. We have before us the alpha of this danger. The omega will be of a more startling nature". Ibid., 16.

"When men standing in the position of leaders and teachers work under the power of spiritualistic ideas and sophistries, shall we keep silent for fear of injuring their influence, while souls are being beguiled?... Those who feel so very peaceable in regard to the works of the men who are spoiling the faith of the people of God, are guided by a delusive sentiment" Ibid., p.9,11.

"Renewed energy is now needed. Vigilant action is called for. Indifference and sloth will result in the loss of personal religion and of heaven... My message to you is: No longer consent to listen without protest to the perversion of truth. We must firmly refuse to be drawn away from the platform of eternal truth, which since 1844 has stood the test" Ibid., p.14,15,50.

"I hesitated and delayed about the sending out of that which the Spirit of the Lord impelled me to write. I did not want to be compelled to present the misleading influence of these sophistries. But in the providence of God, the errors that have been coming in must be met" Ibid., p.55.

"What influence is it that would lead men

at this stage of our history to work in an underhanded, powerful way to tear down the foundation
of our faith – the foundation that was laid at
the beginning of our work by prayerful study
of the word and by relevation? Upon this foundation
we have been building the past fifty years. Do
you wonder that when I see the beginning of
a work that would remove some of the pillars
of our faith, I have something to say? I must
obey the command, 'Meet it'" Ibid., p.58.

All this was written to meet the apostasy
in the alpha period. We are now in the omega
period which Sister White said would come, and
which would be of a "startling nature." And
the words are even more applicable now than
then. Is the reader one of "those who feel so
very peaceable in regard to the works of the
men who are spoiling the faith of the people
of God? Ibid., 11. "Shall we keep silent for
fear of injuring their influence, while souls
are being beguiled?" Ibid.9. It is time to stand
up and be counted. There are times when I have
been tempted to think that I stood alone as
did Elijah. But God told him that there were
7000 others. There are more than that now, thank
God. They need to reveal themselves – and they are
doing it. Most heartening are the letters I
am receiving. It is with deep regret that I
find I am unable to enter into extended correspondence. I am overwhelmed with work.

Christ's death on the cross corresponds to
the moment when on the day of atonement the
high priest had just killed the Lord's goat
in the court. The death of the goat was necessary
for without its blood there could be no atonement.
But death in and of itself was not the atonement, though it was the first and necessary
step. Sister White speaks of the "atonement

commenced on earth" Spirit of Prophecy Vol.3:261. Says Scripture: "It is the blood that maketh atonement" Lev.17:11. And, of course, there could be no blood until after the death had taken place. Without a blood ministration the people would be in the same position as those who on the passover slew the lamb but failed to place the blood on the door posts. "When I see the blood" said God, "I will pass over you" Ex.12:13. The death was useless without the ministration of the blood. It was the blood that counted.

It is the blood that is to be applied, not "an act," "a great act," "sacrificial act," "atoning act," "the act of the cross," "the benefits of the act of the cross," "the benefits of the atonement," all of which expressions are used in "Questions On Doctrine", but any reference to the blood is carefully avoided. It is not an act of any kind that is to be applied. It is the blood. Yet in all the 100 pages in the book dealing with the atonement, not once is the blood spoken of as being applied, or ministered. Can this be merely an oversight, or is it intended? Are we teaching a bloodless atonement? Elder Nichol states the Adventist position correctly when he says, "We believe that Christ's work of atonement was begun rather than completed on Calvary." Answers to Objections p.408. This was published in 1952. We shall be interested to see what the new edition will say. Many are waiting to find out what they are to believe on this important question.

### Blood Atonement

Here are some expressions from the Spirit of Prophecy in regard to blood atonement:
"Jesus was clothed with priestly garments.

He gazed inpity on the remnant, and with a loud
voice of deep pity cried, 'My blood Father; My
blood; My blood; My blood' "Early Writings"p.38.

"He appears in the presence of God as our
great High Priest, ready to accept the repentance
and to answer the prayers of His people, and,
through the merits of His own righteousness,
present them to the Father. He raises His wounded
hands to God, and claims their blood bought
pardon. I have graven them on the palms of My
hands, He pleads. Those memorial wounds of My
humiliation and anguish secure to My church
the best gifts of omnipotence" "Spirit of Prophecy"
Vol. 3, p.261,262.

"The ark that enshrines the tables of the
law is covered with the mercy seat, before which
Christ pleads His blood in the sinner's behalf"
"Great Controversy" p.415.

"When in the typical service the high priest
left the holy place on the day of atonement,
He went in before God to present the blood of
the sin-offering, in behalf of all Israel who
truly repented of their sins. So Christ had
only completed one part of His work as our intercessor, to enter upon another portion of the
work, and He still pleaded His blood before
the Father in behalf of sinners" Ibid., p.429.

Christ is "now officiating before the ark
of God, pleading His bloor in behalf of sinners"
Ibid., p.433.

"Christ, the great high priest, pleading His
blood before the Father in the sinner's behalf,
bears upon His heart the name of every repentant
believing soul" Patriarchs & Prophets" p.351.

"As Christ at His ascension appears in the
presence of God to plead His blood in behalf
of penitent believers, so the priest in the
daily ministration sprinkled the blood of the

sacrifice in the holy place in the sinner's behalf," "Patriarchs & Prophets" p.357.

"The blood of Christ, while it was to release the repentant sinner from the condemnation of the law, was not to cancel the sin; it was to stand on record in the sanctuary until the final atonement," "Patriarchs & Prophets" p.357.

And with all these statements before him, not once does the author of "Questions On Doctrine" mention the blood as being applied or ministered.

### The Final Atonement

"The Father ratified the covenant made with Christ, that He would receive repentant and obedient men, and would love them even as He loves His Son." This as stated above, was on the condition that "Christ was to complete His work and fulfil His pledge to make a man more precious than fine gold, even a man than the golden wedge of ophir." "Desire of Ages" p.790. "This Christ guarantees," "Spirit of Prophecy" Vol. 3, p.250.

When Christ says in His high priestly prayer, "I have finished the work which Thou gavest me to do" (John 17:4). Sister White comments: "He had wrought out a righteous character on earth as an example for man to follow." "Spirit of Prophecy" Vol. 3, p.260.

In working out this righteous character, Christ demonstrated that it could be done. But could others do the same? That needed to be demonstrated also. Christ had guaranteed it could. It was now for Christ to make good His pledge.

Character is not created. It is made; it is developed; it is built through manifold tests and temptations and trials. God at first gives a light test, then a little stronger, and still a little stronger. Little by little resistance to temptations grows stronger, and after a while certain temptations cease to be temptations. A man may have a great struggle with tobacco; but at last he is victorious, and his victory may be so complete that tobacco is a temptation no longer.

Thus, ideally, it should be with every temptation. Holiness is not attained in a day. "Redemption is that process by which the soul is trained for heaven" "Desire of Ages" p. 330. A man may gain victories every day, but still may not have attained. Even Paul had to admit that he had not "already attained, either were already perfect." But undaunted He exclaims, "I follow after that I may apprehend that for which also I am apprehended of Jesus Christ." Philippians 3:12.

Christ had pledged to make man "finer than gold, even the golden wedge of ophir." In this work man must not be a submissive instrument only; he must take an active part. Note these quotations:

"The ransom of the human race was appointed to give man another trial" Ms. 14, 1898. "The plan of salvation was designed to redeem the fallen race, to give man another trial." Signs of the Times, Apr. 26,1899. God "looked upon the victim expiring on the cross and said, 'It is finished; the human race shall have another trial' "Youth's Instructor, June 21, 1900. "That the transgressor might have another trial...the eternal Son of God interposed Himself to bear the punishment of transgression." Review & Herald Feb. 8, 1898. "He suffered in our stead that men could have another test and trial." Special Instruction Relating to the Review & Herald Office, page 28. "As Jesus was accepted as our substitute and surety, every one of us will be accepted if we stand the test and trial for ourselves." Review & Herald June 10, 1890. "The Saviour overcame to show man how he may overcome." "Man must work with his human power aided by the divine power of Christ, to resist and to conquer at any cost to himself. In short, he must overcome as Christ overcame... Man must do his part; he must be victor on his own account, through the strength and grace that Christ gives him." Testimonies, Vol. 4, p.32,33.

Christ had pledged to make men overcomers; He had "guaranteed" this. It was no easy task; but the work of atonement was not finished until and unless He did it. And so Christ persevered till His task should be done. Out of the last generation, out of the weakest of the weak, Christ selects a group with which to make the demonstration that man can overcome as Christ overcame. In the 144,000 Christ will stand just-ified and glorified. They prove that it is pos-sible for man to live a life pleasing to God under all conditions, and that men can at last stand "in the sight of a holy God without an intercessor." "Great Controversy" p.614. The testimony is given them, "they have stood without an intercessor through the final outpouring of God's judgments" "Great Controversy" p.649. "They are the chosen ones, joint heirs with Christ in the great firm of heaven. They overcame, as He overcame" Ms. Nov. 28, 1897. To us comes the invitation "Now, while our High Priest is making atonement for us, we should seek to become perfect in Christ" "Great Controversy" p.623.

## A Mystery

In his epistle to the Ephesians, Paul presents us with a mystery. Says he "For this cause shall a man leave his father and his mother and shall

be joined unto his wife, and the two shall be
one flesh. This is a great mystery; but I speak
concerning Christ and the church" Eph. 5:31,32.
Marriage fitly represents the union between
Christ and the church, effected by the atonement.
In harmony with this picture of a marriage,
the public announcement is made at the close
of probation; "The marriage of the Lamb is come,
and His wife has made herself ready... And to
her it was granted that she should be arrayed
in linen, clean and white; for the linen is
the righteousness of the saints" Rev.19:8. As
husband and wife are one, so now are Christ
and the church. The at-one-ment, the true atonement, the final atonement, the complete atonement
has been made. "The family of heaven and the
family of earth are one." "Desire of Ages" p.835.

### The 144,000

Practically all Adventists have read the last
few chapters in Great Controversy, which describes
the fearful struggle through which God's people
will pass before the end. As Christ was tried
to the utmost in the temptation in the wilderness
and in the garden of Gethsemane, so the 144,000
will likewise be tried. They will apparently
be left to perish, as their prayers remain un-
answered as were Christ's in Gethsemane when
His petitions were denied. But their faith will
not fail. With Job they exclaim, "Though He
slay me, yet will I trust Him." Job 13:15.

The final demonstration of what God can do
in humanity is made in the last generation who
bears all the infirmities and weaknesses which
the race has acquired through six thousand years
of sin and transgression. In the words of Sister
White they bore "the results of the working
of the great law of heredity" "Desire of Ages" p.49.

The weakest of mankind are to be subjected to the strongest of Satan's temptations, that the power of God might be abundantly shown. "It was an hour of fearful terrible agony to the saints. Day and night they cried unto God for deliverance. To outward appearance, there was no possibility of their escape." "Early Writings" p. 283.

According to the new theology which our leaders have accepted and are now teaching, the 144,000 will be subjected to a temptation immeasurably stronger than any Christ ever experienced. For while the last generation will bear the weaknesses and passions of their forefathers, they claim that Christ was exempt from all these. Christ, we are told, did not inherit any of the passions "that corrupt the natural descendants of Adam." "Questions On Doctrine" p.383. He was therefore functioning on a higher and altogether different level from men who have to battle with inherited passions and hence He does not know and has not experienced the real power of sin. But this is not the kind of Saviour I need. I need One who has been "tempted in all points like as we are" Heb. 4:15. The "substitute Christ" which our leaders present to us, I must reject and do reject. Thank God, "we have not a high priest which cannot be touched with the feeling of our infirmities, but was in all points tempted like as we are, yet without sin." Ibid.

## Indictment Against God

But more than even this is involved in the new theology; it places an indictment against God as the author of a scheme to deceive both men and Satan. Here is the situation:

Satan has consistently maintained that God is unjust in requiring men to obey His law, which he claims is impossible. God has maintained that it can be done, and to substantiate His claim, offered to send His Son to this world to prove His contention. The Son did come and kept the law and challenged men to convince Him of sin. He was found to be sinless, holy and without blame. He proved that the law could be kept, and God stood vindicated; and His requirement that men keep His commandments was found to be just. God had won, and Satan was defeated.

But there was a hitch in this; for Satan claimed that God had not played fair; He had favoured His Son, had "exempted" Him from the results of the working of the great law of heredity to which all other men were subject; He had exempted Christ "from the inherited passions and pollutions that corrupt the natural descendants of Adam." "Questions On Doctrine" p.383. He had not exempted mankind in general, but Christ only. That of course, invalidated Christ's work on earth. He was no longer one of us who had demonstrated the power of God to keep men from sinning. He was a deceiver whom God had given preferred treatment and was not afflicted with inherited passions as men are.

Satan had little difficulty in having men accept this view; the Catholic church accepted it; in due time, the evangelicals gave their consent; and in 1956 the leaders of the Adventist church also adopted this view. It was the matter of "exemption" that caused Peter to take Christ aside and say, "Be it far from thee, Lord; this shall not be unto thee," which so raised the wrath of Christ that He told Peter, "Get thee behind me, Satan" Matt. 16:22,23. Christ did not want to be exempt. He told Peter, "Thou savourest not the things that be of God." So some today savour not the things of God. They think it merely a matter of semantics. God pity such and open their eyes to the things that be of God. With the surrender of the Adventist leaders to the monstrous-doctrine of an "exempt" Christ, Satan's last opposition has surrendered. We pray again, may God save His people.

I have been asked what I expect to accomplish. I am not out to "win" any argument. I am a Seventh-day Adventist minister whose work is to preach the truth and combat error. The Bible is mostly a record of the protest of God's witnesses against the prevailing sins of the church, and also of their apparent failure. Practically all protesters sealed their testimony with their blood, and the church went on until God intervened. All Paul hoped was that he might "save some" 1 Cor. 9:22. Practically all the apostles died martyrs, and Christ they hanged on a tree. It took forty years before the destruction came. But when God intervened He did thorough work. This denomination needs to go back to the instruction given in 1888, which was scorned. We need a reform in organization that will not permit a few men to direct every move made anywhere in the world. We need a reform that will not permit a few men to handle finances as is now being done. We need a reform that will not permit men to spend millions on institutions not authorized by the vote of the constituency, while mission fields are suffering for want of the barest necessities. We need a change in the emphasis that is given to promotion, finances and statistics. We need to restore the Sabbath School to its rightful place in the work of God. We need to put a stop to the entertainments and suppers that are creeping in under the guise of raising money for good purposes. We need to put a stop to the weekly announcements in church that are merely disguised advertisements. This list could be greatly enlarged.

But all these, while important, are after all only minor things. We need a reformation and revival most of all. If our leaders will not lead in this, "then shall there enlargement and deliverance arise to the Jews from another place." Esther 4:14. I am of good cheer, praying for the peace of Israel.

## The Biblical Research Institute (Australasia)
### Article in The Anchor Magazine, Feb. 1986

In February 1976, when Dr Ford's theology was investigated by the B.R.I., he himself was a member of the Institute. Normal ethics were dispensed with for his membership was not suspended while his doctrinal positions were investigated. Such conduct lends credence to the feelings of some of the 'Concerned Brethren' who felt it was, in fact, **their** positions which had come under question. The points of issue were as follows:

**1.     The Nature of Salvation and Righteousness by Faith** - Dr Ford claimed that obedience to the Decalogue under the power of the Holy Spirit was not possible prior to glorification. He further claimed that sanctification was not part of the Gospel message. This easily demonstrable false stand was opposed in papers presented by Pr Frank Basham and Dr John Clifford.

**2.     The Sanctuary Message** - Dr Ford claimed that the Atonement was completed at the cross and that Jesus entered the Most Holy place in A.D.31, rather than in 1844. These were the main issues upon which Dr Ford was later dismissed following the investigations of the Glacier View meetings. Pastor Burnside most perceptively demonstrated the non-Scriptural basis of Dr Ford's position.

**3.     The Age of the Earth** - Dr Ford taught that creation week occurred thousands of years in excess of the approximately six thousand years testified to in Scripture and the Spirit of Prophecy. Dr Russell Standish presented the Bible and the Spirit of Prophecy truth on this matter.

246

**4. The Infallibility of the Bible** - Dr Ford taught that there were many errors of fact concerning science, history, genealogies etc. in Scripture, while stating it was free of error in setting forth the path to salvation. Pr Frank Breaden had little difficulty in overthrowing Dr Ford's error on this point. Eventually, only three matters were considered by the Bible Research Institute - viz. the Sanctuary message, the Age of the Earth and the Infallibility of Scripture.

### THE VERDICT

Dr Ford was exonerated of heresy solely on the grounds that "reference to majority positions taken by current S.D.A. authors and scholars" upheld his positions.

Sometime later, when it was pointed out that this must surely be the first time in which doctrines were accepted on the basis of what some authors and scholars believed, an amendment to the original finding was hurriedly made. It added the Bible and the Spirit of Prophecy to the authority of the scholars.

Such equivocation only served to exacerbate the dilemma of the B.R.I., for it would be difficult to imagine anything more futile than to attempt to use the Bible and the Spirit of Prophecy to prove the earth is considerably older than six thousand years.

Surely, we are talking about the greatest retraction of truth ever undertaken by any leadership in any Division! These people then returned to their positions of trust in leadership of the Division and in the Theology Department of Avondale College.

It would be indeed reassuring if the leadership of the South Pacific Division on the occasion of this 10th anniversary were to:

**1.** Have the B.R.I. publicly reverse its find-ings in the 'Record' or the 'Review', stating concisely and precisely where and why Dr Ford was wrong in each issue listed above.

**2.** Re-affirm the message of the third angel of Rev. 14 as the message entrusted to the Remnant Church and identify the 'beast' as the papacy and 'his image' as apostate Protestantism.

Should the leadership deem the foregoing account of the B.R.I. proceedings to be inaccurate and our suggestions unreasonable, let them now justify such a position by releasing copies of the un-expurgated tapes of the meetings to the brethren concerned, as initially promised.

Failure to do so will leave our Church in an official state of apostasy, and the leadership will continue to be seen to condone and encourage heresy.

**Author's NOTE:** As at the time this book was written, no official response to this appeal has been forthcoming. For the record, the names of the participants in the 1976 B.R.I. meetings are listed below:

**ADMINISTRATION:**

Pr. C. Adams, Conference President
Pr. D. Bain, Division Health Director
Pr. C. Barritt, Conference President
Pr. C. Christian, Conference President
Dr. D. Ford, Chairman, Avondale Theology Department
Pr. R. Frame, Division President
Pr. A. Jorgensen, B.R.I. & Field Secretary
Pr. C. Judd, T.T.U. Conference President
Dr. E. Magnusson, Principal, Avondale College
Pr. R. Moe, Conference President
Pr. L. Naden, Retired Division President
Pr. K. Parmenter, Division Secretary

Pr. R. Parr, Editor 'Signs of the Times'
Dr. A. Patrick, Theology Lecturer, Avondale College
Dr. A. Salom, Church Pastor, Wahroonga
Pr. R. Stanley, Division Ministerial Secretary
Pr. A. Tolhurst, Conference President
Pr. L. Tolhurst, Theology Lecturer, Avondale College
Pr. S. Uttley, T.A.U. Conference President
Dr. N. Young, Theology Lecturer, Avondale College

**CONCERNED MEMBERS:**

Pr. O.K. Anderson, retired Evangelist
Pr. F. Basham, retired Church Pastor
Pr. F. Breaden, retired Church Pastor
Pr. G. Burnside, retired Evangelist
Dr. G. Clifford, Layman
Pr. R. Heggie, retired Mission President
Pr. A. Jacobsen, retired Mission President
Pr. L. Jones, retired Evangelist
Pr. J. Keith retired Union & Mission President
Pr. J. Kent, retired Evangelist
Pr. A. Knight, retired Bible Teacher
Br. R. Marks, Layman
Pr. E. Martin, retired Missionary
Br. H. Reed, Layman
Dr. R. Standish, Layman
Br. F. Williams, Layman

(As one who believes that we are all account-
able to our Maker in the great day of God's
judgment, the writer feels it his duty to make
the following facts known regarding the late
Pr S.M. Uttley who at the time of the B.R.I.
meetings was President of the Trans-Tasman Union
Conference. He therefore, was among the Administrators who took part in the B.R.I. meetings
of February, 1976.)
Prior to publication of the above account
of the B.R.I. meetings in the Anchor, the author
who was the editor of the Anchor magazine submit-

ted the script to Pr. S. Uttley for comment. Pr Uttley claimed that his recollections of the meetings were hazy, but he was adamant that Desmond Ford had "pulled the wool over their (the Administration's) eyes." He could see nothing in the article which he felt needed correcting. At this time, he claimed that he was quite aware that much of Ford's beliefs were still being taught at Avondale College, naming one Theology Lecturer in particular, who was at the B.R.I. meetings.

**Pastor Raymond Stanley's APPEAL TO THE B.R.I. EYE WITNESS ACCOUNT,** Printed in Anchor July 1986

It is a matter of easily-verifiable historical record that on February 3 and 4 of 1976, the members of the Australasian B.R.I. (Biblical Research Institute) met with a group of ministers and laymen at Avondale and Wahroonga to hear allegations of doctrinal deviations against Desmond Ford and his answer to the allegations.

The February 3 meeting was held at Avondale College and the February 4 meeting was held at the Division Office, Wahroonga. Pastor Robert Frame was Chairman and a complete tape-recording was made of the papers presented, the replies given and the general discussion.

Papers presented by the Field men sought to uphold the traditional, published Sanctuary teachings of Seventh-day Adventists - especially the positions set forth in the Ellen G White writings - which affirm:

1.    A real sanctuary in heaven with two segments or apartments - corresponding with the "holy place" and the "most holy place" of the earthly sanctuary.

2.    Christ's two-phased ministry in the heavenly

sanctuary, corresponding with the "daily service" and the "yearly service" on earth.

3.    Christ's "first apartment" ministry beginning at His ascension in A.D.31 and His "second apartment" ministry beginning in A.D.1844 at the end of the 2,300 prophetic "days" of Daniel 8:14.

Dr Ford's replies showed that he did, indeed, deviate radically from traditional Seventh-day Adventism regarding its long-held and widely published Sanctuary doctrine. He was especially emphatic and explicit in his rejection of a heavenly sanctuary with "two apartments" and his repudiation of published Adventist positions became more and more evident as the meeting proceeded.

One curious – even baffling – circumstance was the apparent approval and acceptance of Dr Ford's denials of historic S.D.A. faith, by the B.R.I. members, which of course, included the Division Officers and some other administrators. **Certainly they made no outcry against Desmond Ford's denials.** The very silence of the Division administrators represented endorsement. While there was vocal, emphatic, unequivocal disapproval of Dr Ford's views by the Field men, there was no corresponding disapproval from the B.R.I. members **with one conspicuous exception.**

During the second session held at Wahroonga on February 4, Pastor Raymond Stanley, then Division Ministerial Association Secretary, and a member of the B.R.I. rose to his feet, addressed the chair and asked permission to speak. He held up a copy of the S.D.A. **Baptismal Certificate,** which contains a condensed summary of our Church's doctrines, and is "official" in the sense that since 1931 it has been repeatedly endorsed by plenary sessions of the General Conference.

Pastor Stanley then read the full text of Article 8 of the **Baptismal Certificate,** which says:

"Upon His ascension, Christ began His ministry as High Priest in the holy place of the heavenly sanctuary, which sanctuary is the antitype of the earthly tabernacle of the former dispensation. A work of investigative judgment began as Christ entered the second pase of His ministry, in the most holy place, foreshadowed in the earthly service by the Day of Atonement. This work of the investigative judgment in the heavenly sanctuary began in 1844, at the close of the 2,300 years, and will end with the close of probation. Heb. 4:14; 8:1,2; Lev. 16:2,29; Heb. 9:23,24; Dan. 8:14; 9:24-27; Rev. 14:6,7; 22:11."

Pastor Stanley commented that while he felt bound to adhere to this Article, he was unable to reconcile this official doctrinal statement with what he had heard from Dr Ford and he appealed for help in his dilemma.

The saddest fact of all was that Pastor Stanley's poignant appeal for guidance went over like a "lead balloon." There was dead silence from the members of the B.R.I. **Not one of the Division administrators sprang to his feet and voiced support for Pastor Stanley and/or opposition to Dr. Ford.** Not one of the College theologians sprang to his feet to do the same. The B.R.I. members seemed like men bewitched. **They were as still as statues and as silent as the grave.**

Is it any wonder that our Division leaders have lost credibility in the eyes of faithful and loyal ministers and members? Here is a case where our Australasian leaders, in the presence of many witnesses, **refused pointblank to declare** their loyalty to their own denominational Baptismal Certificate! And yet they - in common with every church member - have solemnly taken Baptismal vows, and thus pledged themselves to observe and defend these precious Articles of our historic faith!

## Condition of the Ministry in Australasia.
## Letter to Australasian Division President from the late Pr. W.M.R. Scragg, 24 Sept. 1978

Thank you for your circular. You surely are moving around your parish.

I had a long letter from Walter in which he wrote up again his views on Righteousness by Faith. He told how he had attended a meeting on this subject a few weeks ago bringing together our top theologians and administrators. He said that Elder Pierson, Wood, and another contended for our old views while the theologians for the new. He rather sided with the new. In his letter of four large pages he wrote up the new. I read it carefully and then turned him to Hosea 7:8 which tells of Ephraim mixing himself with the people and his being a cake not turned. I wrote him that was what he had set up "a cake not turned." Baked on one side and left doughy on the other.

We cannot have Righeousness by Faith without repentance. Repentance means true sorrow for sin and the power to be converted and turned to righteous living.

In your circular you wrote of evangelism in this home field of 17,000,000 people. Think of it, 2,000 baptised last year for a years work in the home field. What a dearth for the year! Minus the apostasies and those who died in the home field? I shall state here the reason that has caused such poor success:-

1. Many of our theologians have not been successful evangelists, therefore they have not passed on to our young men experiences gathered from their own endeavours to win souls.

2. The downright rubbish that has been passed onto them under their lecturers.

**3.**   The casting off of the old teachings of Sr. White and Uriah Smith on such subjects as Armageddon, the King of the North, the Struggle between Capital and Labour, the Jew and the Arab in Prophecy etc.

**4.**   The fact that because of our vast involvement in business and public collecting for money, we have softened down our attack on Apostasy and **we are** not giving the Message with a loud cry. We are afraid to prejudice the public in these two areas stated above.

**5.**   Our preaching and our lecturing to the public is too apologetic in a general way.

**6.**   The motor car has made, on a large scale, our workers lazy.

**7.**   Our leaders and teachers do not set an example in soul-winning. They sit too much on their hind quarters when they could be out giving studies. Every worker from the G.C. President down to the boy who sweeps the office should strive to win souls. On a whole our workers talk of the Second Coming with their tongue in their cheek. They don't really believe that Christ's coming is near. Many are poor watchmen such as stated in Isa. 56:10. Actions speak louder than words.

Think it through; two thousand baptisms would be about on an average of two souls to each worker and nothing from 47,000 members and I should add the number of about 10,000 young people.
Think of the aids we have today re television and radio programmes. The Five Day Plans and health units operating, of some 40,000 Signs or more a month in circulation etc., etc.
I led out as a President for twenty-two years

and I know I had to get after the workers hot and strong to get them up and at it. If I were in your place I do not think I would take things as complacently as you are writing.

Where is the fire that characterised our old workers? We have had three workers here the last ten years and you could count on the fingers of one hand the number who have been brought in by them from the public.

Enormous tithes are coming to our treasury and it would seem that it is costing 15,000 dollars to win a soul throughout Australia and New Zealand. Workers have their eyes on the building of homes for the future more than the mansions above.

Brother ... it is by the "foolishness of preaching" that souls are stirred and won. We need the J.W. Kents, the Roy Andersons, the George Burnsides to be resurrected today to help us out. We should have a strong evangelist in every city leading out a good team, in a mighty preaching of the Word. Outstanding evangelists are scarcer than presidents. We are over administered today. Too many money changers in the house of God. Pray for Christ to send the Holy Spirit to ship them out to soul-winning evangelism before He returns. We need another Sr. White right now. Please be concerned over the dearth in souls being won.

Our task is to win a remnant multitude to close the work of God. See Dan. 8:14,26; Dan. 12:4; Rev. 10:11; Rev. 14:6; Rev. 7:9. These texts point us to our responsibility.

We are in the world to finish the task of soul-winning.

Sr. White wrote that a thousand will come in a day. This brushes the 144,000 aside. Let us set our sights on 144,000,000.

256

By my understanding of Rev. 13:11-18 we are not near the finished work. Some of our outstanding prophecies are not yet in sight of being fulfilled.

You are the leader in this field and God will hold you responsible.

Well, God bless and cheer you on to do your duty, Yours for an abundance of souls.

**Larrie B Kostenko - "The Human Nature
of Christ in S.D.A. Christology"**
Portion of Research Paper - Andrews University
S.D.A. Theological Seminary, 1982.

### Chapter 3 - CONCLUSION

The concept of the human nature of Christ
that continually and completely characterized
S.D.A. theology from the 1880's through the
1940's originated at least as early as 1874 -
1875 in the writings of Ellen G White. E.J.
Waggoner and A.T. Jones championed this view
from the 1880's through the early 1900's. Ellen
White's unequivocal support of their (and her)
view explains the fact that this view continues
within Adventism even today--notwithstanding
wishful statements to the contrary by men such
as Anderson and Froom.

Seventh-day Adventists have always held that
Christ in His human nature was sinless. Originally, this was understood to mean that Christ,
who took **our** humanity, so depended on and was
linked to divine power that He **lived** sinlessly.
The fact that Christ took **our** humanity was emphasized to mean that He is our **example**. The incarnation of Christ in fallen humanity supplies
the need of fallen man for divine power in order
to overcome Satan.

In the 1950's, some of our leading men began
introducing the terminology and concepts of
original sin. Sin was no longer identified solely
with "character," "life," and "morality." Sin
is defined as something one inherits at birth.
Christ was "born holy." We are not. His body
"was free from the taint of sin." Ours are not.
Christ had no "inborn sin." We do. The result
of the introduction of this view of sin was
the denial that Christ was in all points tempted

like as we are.

This new view did not, however, meet with unanimous acceptance. Even while it was being introduced, the older view was published in our magazine--sometimes in the same issue.

Robert Brinsmead was used to champion the historic view in 1964. However, as Brinsmead sharpened his doctrine of original sin, he capitulated to the new view by 1973. As he applied the doctrine of original sin systematically to other distinctive doctrines, he repudiated one by one the judgment, the law, and the Sabbath.

It is significant that the doctrine of original sin was an issue at the 1901 General Conference. Under the leadership of E.J. Waggoner and Ellen G. White, it, and the view that Christ took prelapsarian human nature were both repudiated. Only the sponsorship of Ellen G. White explains the fact that this view of the humanity of Christ gained such prominence in S.D.A. theology. Jones and Waggoner would not have gotten off the ground in 1888 were it not for her support. It is significant that she never once rebuked them privately or publicly for their view on the humanity of Christ. A survey of the index cards (in the E.G. White vault) of her letters to them reveals that she was well able to rebuke them on many personal matters as well as theological ones. But she never once corrected them for a faulty view of the humanity of Christ.

The new view was not only the result, however, of absorbing the terminology and concepts of original sin. It is clear that Adventist leadership was intent on rectifying an impaired Adventist image. The desire to avoid being called a cult and gain acceptance in the evangelical world was a top priority. This motivation is praiseworthy. However, it seems sad that what was intended to accomplish greater influence of the church has resulted in impoverishing her historic doctrines.

Desmond Ford was a seminary student in Washington D.C. at the time of this Christological turmoil in 1958. He was to intensify its emphasis of the new view in the late 1970's and early 1980's. This intensification led Ford so far outside historic Adventism that he was defrocked.

Another effect of the new view within Adventist scholarship and thought is denial of Christian perfection. This concept of which Ellen G. White wrote so much about has become a matter of embarrassment for many Adventists.

In 1978 the writer of this paper authored a research paper on perfection in the thought of Ellen G. White. When he presented it to a seminar of senior theology majors at Walla Walla College, the thesis that God expects moral perfection of His followers was ill-received. Having read the paper of E.G. White quotes, the instructor seemed surprised, but countered "What about Scripture sources to support this view?" In addition he added that my view of sin was "superficial." He defined perfection as "maturity within a relationship"--a view that originates from Edward Heppenstall, one whom Paxton identifies as accepting the doctrine of original sin and denying perfection.

The whole point of mentioning this incident is to illustrate some of the effects that changing our doctrines of sin and Christ can have on how we accept the authority of E.G. White and how we come to regard other historic Seventh-day Adventist doctrines.

### Dr R.R. Standish on Rumour Spreading.
### Letter to Pr. Walter Scragg, President
### South Pacific Division, February 28, 1989

I have just read a letter from my esteemed brother-in-law, Dr David Pennington. In it I learned for the first time that senior Division leadership had circulated, verbally and in writing false and damaging rumour that my dear brother, Colin, had been relieved of his sacred ministerial credentials for misbehaviour.

May our heavenly Father forgive you and your fellow leaders who exulted over the "news." This is the second major false rumour that has been issued from your office. Each time you place responsibility for your actions upon the General Conference. But you have a personal responsibility too. The first was the utterly unfounded assertion that the Hartland Team had taken 800,000 guilders out of the Netherlands. I have never heard that a written correction was made when the facts were obtained and you discovered that the figure had been inflated one thousand fold. One such mistake would surely have cautioned care in the future.

Is it the practice of the Division Secretariat to send throughout the Unions and Conferences details of each case of pastors whose credentials are removed?

When a man forfeits his ministerial calling by his conduct, it is a matter of the greatest heartache to God's people. It is not a matter over which we rejoice, nor which we hasten to spread without confirmation, from one corner of a Division to the other. May I be bold to suggest that this is not the way to treat one of the sons of your Division even if the gossip had been correct. Would not it have been a more Christian course to have expressed sorrow and concern and to have requested the North American Division for details of their decision? In this case, had such a proper procedure been followed, your administration would have ascertained the true situation and would have spared itself a shameful episode.

None had expressed deeper concern for the teaching of Dr Ford than had Colin and I. Yet the day I learnt that he had been relieved of his credentials, tears of deep sorrow welled up in my eyes. We did not exultantly send the news far and wide. God can testify to that. Our true emotions were expressed in writing. There was no gilding of the truth: they were and remain our true sentiments. "As the inevitable procession was taken through Glacier View, disavowal of Dr Ford's teachings, loss of credentials and finally annulment of his ordination, we watched with gnawing anguish of heart. While we could not fault the decisions of our brethren in these matters, none of this altered our vision of a man seen over thirty years previously through the eyes of admiring sixteen-year-olds. To us Des was still the old college mate, the youth bursting with potential; still the man of unmeasurable God-bestowed talents; the supreme orator; the quick-silver debator; but most of all, as ourselves, a man so in need of the very truths which he saw fit to reject. No doctrinal disagreement could remove from our hearts the bond of Christian charity we held for Des.

"And it is the human tragedy of the **new theology** which impels us to write, lest others be snared by its errors. While Des is the most notable,the most visable casualty of the **new theology** others just as precious to their Redeemer and to their loved ones have imbibed its philosophies" (**Adventism Challenged, Vol. A,**

**pp. 26,27).**

Walter, I fear lest you find yourself in this latter situation. Your dear father, my first Conference President as a new worker in 1952, loved you dearly and he expressed his concern for your doctrinal bent a few years before his death. In a letter to the man who then held your position, he stated (September 24, 1978), "I had a letter from Walter in which he wrote up again his views on Righteousness by Faith. He told me how he had attended a meeting on this subject a few weeks ago bringing together our top theologians and administrators. He said that Elders Pierson, Wood and another contended for our old view while the theologians for the new view. He rather sided with the new. In his letter of four large pages, he wrote up the new. I read it carefully and then turned him to Hosea 7:8 which tells of Ephraim mixing himself with the people and him being a cake not turned. I wrote him that that was what he had set up "a cake not turned." "Baked on one side and left doughy on the other."

Walter, if you had heeded the godly counsel of your father you would now not be fighting every dedicated preacher of truth but uplifting their hands as they preach their mighty messages centred upon God's Word.

For too long, men of the calibre of Pastor Burnside, Pastor Anderson, Pastor Cooke, Pastor Jacobson, Pastor Keith, Pastor Ball, Pastor Breaden, Pastor Kent, Pastor Heggie, Pastor White, Pastor Knight, Pastor Basham, Pastor Jones, Pastor Martin, Pastor Needham, Pastor Ferris and others have felt the full fury of the ecclesiastical wrath of the South Pacific Division leadership. Yet God's record of the lives of this noble band of men of God will prove entirely different.

Your course is wrong. It is a discouragement to many and a snare to others. Walter, I dearly wish to spend eternity with you. Please, for the sake of the One who died for you and put you in such a position of leadership as a shepherd of His flock, alter the course that you have set against God's servants who uplift truth.

Your leadership is an encouragement to Conference Presidents to follow your example. How quickly the President of the Western Australian Conference, perhaps the most controversial appointment ever to a Conference Presidency in the Division, has spread widely both the false reports you have circulated. He thought he could trust your word. It has quite unnecessarily brought him into terrible disrepute amongst his flock.

Indeed this whole episode has brought great anguish and terrible distrust of you personally and the entire Division leadership. This causes me no little anguish. Had the rumour been true, it would have fermented similar emotions, but that it contains no veracity whatsoever has heaped coals of fire upon the situation. May our God return peace and divine purpose once more to our Division. I love God's church. I love the brethren. I am a Seventh-day Adventist to the marrow of my bones. I have dedicated every fibre of my soul to its cause and our Saviour. I am devastated that you continue to see it as your mission to follow this course. I pray God that He will show you a better way.

There is so much in our Australasian church which needs our prayers and fervent efforts to reform. Apostasy is rampaging through the church. Dancing at socials, charismatic activities rock music in churches, secular and even sacrilegious music (e.g. Jesus Christ Superstar theme) presented in our churches, lowered standards, all are on the increase. Truly our church in Australia and New Zealand has never faced such a crisis of truth. Surely these should capture our attention rather than the efforts of God's men to preach the acme of love for Jeus, keeping His commandments. Let us beware for we have been warned that "A refusal to obey the commandments of God, and a determination to cherish hatred against those who proclaim these commandments, leads to the most determined war on the part of the dragon, whose whole energies are brought to bear against the commandment-keeping people of God" (8 Testimonies, p.117).

How I know from thousands of letters and personal meetings that Colin holds a humble commitment. God has used him and will continue to do so. I have no fear of that. Throughout all the efforts to subvert our ministries, God has seen fit to guide us through. I just love Him so much for that.

You will know from the kind defence that my brother-in-law has made, just how deeply our family feels. But one matter I wish to make plain (and I believe I speak for every member of the loyal Standish Seventh-day Adventists); we will hold no grudge. We have freely forgiven. This forgiveness is unconditional. It is not based upon a public retraction. It is extended to all who have spread this rumour, particularly those who have delighted to do so. God help them. It extends to those whose only emotion is one of shame-facedness and to those who are deeply disappointed to learn that the rumour is false. The faith of the members of the Standish family in our Seventh-day Adventist church, both in Australia and world-wide has never wavered nor been stronger. We will ever remain as its dedicated servants.

I wish to share this commitment with our many loyal friends whose faith has been severely tested by this episode. Thus I plan to circulate this letter widely since I wish to encourage those who have felt utter despair in believing the false rumour. I wish them to love God and His church more fully than ever and to rejoice and offer prayers of gratitude that God has once more cared for His servant and preserved His ministry.

May God bless and strengthen you in your ministry for Him. Yours in the blessed hope.

## Pastor David Lin "ON JESUIT INFILTRATION"
### January 27, 1984

One 'rumour' causing concern among Adventists is that there are Jesuit agents among our church officials and educators. It is reported that a Jesuit priest converted to the Baptist faith divulged this information. To assert that it is untrue and unfounded does not satisfy most lay people, simply because it is just as hard to disprove as it is to verify such a story. However, the problem can be studied from another angle. I propose to ask, (1) Is it possible for Jesuit agents to enter our ranks as church officials or educators? And then, (2) Is it probable?

I venture to say that it is entirely possible for secret agents to infiltrate the S.D.A. organization. The following episode during my tenure in office of Secretary of the China Division shows how easily a special Agent of any kind can enter one of our institutions:

In 1950 our Chiaotoushen training school was struggling to keep going with a reduced teaching staff, when word was received that a recent convert baptised in an effort in Hong Kong offered to connect with the school as a teacher of Social Science. The evangelist who recommended him reported that he had a Ph.D degree and would be a real asset to the cause. So the School Board voted to employ the learned Professor. I visited with him after he came. In his photo album I saw pictures of this man dressed in military attire, taken in Italy. But I did not suspect that he was anything but a learned scholar. However, the young people who attended his classes soon nick-named him "Dr Punk" because they had sized him up, and knew that he was just an empty-

headed dumb-bell. But the Head of our school
prized him as the only Ph.D on his staff, even
though no one ventured to examine his diploma.
We just believed what the preacher in Hong Kong
told us. After about a year the true identity
of this 'scholar' came to light. He was a Kuo-
mintan agent engaged in counter-revolutionary
activities. He had even brought a body-guard
disguised as a student. Before his arrest, if
any one had said that there were undercover
political agents in our ranks, I would have
denied it.

But now I've learned to be wiser, because
the fact is, in the face of secret infiltration,
the S.D.A. organization is wholly defenceless.
We have no counter-espionage system, and of
course we don't want one, simply because we
are organized to spread the gospel. But if and
when a secret set up such as the Society of
Jesus makes up its mind to infiltrate us, we
make an easy victim - the easiest in the world.

### IF I WERE A JESUIT CHIEF

Now to the next question: Is it probable?
Considering that the third angel's message is
most effective in exposing the papal man of
sin, and remembering what the Society of Jesus
was founded for, we may safely say that it is
highly probable that the Jesuits have picked
out the S.D.A. church as one of their chief
targets, and even now their secret agents occupy
important posts in our organization.

If I were a modern Jesuit chief, I would certainly regard the Seventh-day Adventists one
of the greatest obstacles to papal ambitions
for papal world supremacy. So I would concentrate
a strong task force to alter the teachings,
cripple the finances, and control the leadership

of this organization. In different parts of the world I would enlist say 10,000 Catholic youth to attend S.D.A. evangelistic efforts, be baptized and then enrol in S.D.A. Colleges and Seminaries. I would instruct them to study hard, graduate with honours and then apply for work as preachers and teachers. They would be taught how to undermine the S.D.A. doctrines, destroy the influence of Ellen White, convert the S.D.A. educational system and sever S.D.A. hospitals. My long-term global programme would have as its goal the complete subversion of the S.D.A. church in one generation. In all this I would have the blessing of the pope and almost limitless funds.

Impossible? Preposterous? Not at all. It is highly probable. In fact the present state of things among us seems to indicate that just such a programme was initiated as early as 1950. I dare say that if the Jesuits are engaged in a less ambitious scheme, they would be unworthy of the Jesuit name, for the oath of the Knights of Columbus binds every Jesuit to destroy all 'heretics' by every possible means.

## IS IT I ?

Another 'rumour' is that our administrative officials are 'tainted with papalism.' Unlike the first 'rumour,' which is a question of fact, this is a matter of opinion. But it is neither untrue nor unfounded, because of certain incidents which would have been unthinkable 40 years ago, but have now become church history, such as 'our' audience with the pope and the gold medallion we presented to him. It is said that when our official representative called on the Roman pontiff, he addressed him as 'holy father.' This detail may be hard to verify, but I dare say it too is highly probable, because many Adventists are already accustomed to address Catholic priests as 'father' so-and-so. So why all the fuss about adding a 'holy' or 'most holy' to it? We are just following accepted social practice. And, anyway, 'pope' and 'papacy' are derived from 'papa.' Perhaps 10 years from now it won't be necessary to deny that we are 'tainted with papalism' as then it will be quite natural for us to admire the pope and call him 'holy father.'

Because there are concerned lay members who would by God's help arrest such a dangerous trend, this 'rumour' is being kept alive. But it should be pointed out that the responsibility for it does not rest with our lay members, but with those who arranged for that audience with the pope. To say that the men who conceived such a move are 'tainted with papalism,' is no exaggeration, and if our leaders have any sense of responsibility toward God and His people they should not attempt to deny or to excuse this shameful 'taint,' but should humble themselves before God and publicly confess that they have offended Him by befriending the power which has spoken blasphemy against the Most High, and is drunken with the blood of His saints. Every true Seventh-day Adventist will refuse to follow the leadership of any man who claims to be a son of God, but in fact honours the man of sin by calling him 'father.'

It is understandable that if the 'rumours' mentioned above continue to be circulated, an air of mutual suspicion will prevail, and the 'morale of leadership' will suffer. But again, we insist that the source of trouble is not the lay people, but the men whose words and actions furnish ground for such rumours. If they continue to make friendly overtures to Babylon and her daughters on the one hand and make 'categorical' denials of any such leanings on the other, the lay people certainly will not be deceived. A sorry state of affairs may develop in which our watchmen must be watched, lest they fail to detect the approach of danger and open the city gates to let the enemy in.

What I present is not fantasy, but reality. We face serious problems. Unfounded rumours need not worry us, but a single 'rumour' arising from historical facts cannot be silenced by a thousand denials. We must ponder the question, 'When the Son of man cometh, shall He find faith on the earth?' Instead of pointing the finger at the supposed source of rumours. let each of us rather ask, "Lord is it I?" Am I in word and deed an unwitting ally of the enemy of souls? Am I among the 'wheat' or the 'chaff?' After all, there were false brethren in the days of the apostles, and 'men of Belial' among the braves who sided with David when he fled from Saul. So it is not strange to discover some traitors among us. Only let every soul determine to be among the 'called, chosen and faithful.' For in every crisis God has His Calebs and Joshuas. Be it Jesuit infiltration or internal apostasy, what should we do about it? Sigh and cry? Yes, but the crying should be confined not to weeping, for the Lord says, 'Cry aloud, spare not, lift up the voice like a trumpet...' Isa. 58:1. 'Not by might, nor by power, but by My Spirit, saith the Lord of hosts,' will He take care of His church and 'thoroughly purge His floor.'"

## ATTACK ON FUNDAMENTAL PRINCIPLES

"He calls upon us to hold firmly, with the grip of faith, to the fundamental principles that are based upon unquestionable authority" E.G. White. Series B, No. 2, p.59, and reprinted in 1 Selected Messages p.208.

In 1872 the Seventh-day Adventist Publishing Association published "A Declaration of the Fundamental Principles" which they taught and practiced. Hence they are the principles which Mrs White claimed were "based upon unquestionable authority".

Because Mrs White singled out "the ministration of Christ in the heavenly sanctuary" and the messages of the three angels of Revelation 14, as those which come under special attack, we here reproduce the relevant Fundamental Principles as published in 1872.

### FUNDAMENTAL PRINCIPLES (1872)

F.P.No. 2.    That there is One Lord Jesus Christ, the Son of the Eternal Father, the one by whom God created all things, and by whom they do consist; that He took on Him the nature of the seed of Abraham for the redemption of our fallen race; that He dwelt among men, full of grace and truth, lived our example, died our sacrifice, and was raised for our justification.

He ascended on high to be our only mediator in the sanctuary in Heaven, where, with His own blood, He makes atonement for our sins; which atonement so far from being made on the cross, which was by the offering of the sacrifice, is the very last portion of His work as priest according to the example of the Levitical priesthood, which foreshadowed and prefigures the ministry of our Lord in Heaven. See Lev.16;

272

Heb. 8:4,5; 9:6,7.

**F.P.No. 10.** That the sanctuary of the new covenant is the tabernacle of God in Heaven, of which Paul speaks in Hebrews 8 and onward, of which our Lord, as great High Priest, is minister; that this sanctuary is the antitype of the work of the Jewish priests of the former dispensation. Heb. 8:1-5; etc.

That this is the sanctuary to be cleansed at the end of the 2300 days, what is termed its cleansing being in this case, as in the type, **simply the entrance of the High Priest into the Most Holy place,** to finish the round of service connected therewith, by blotting out and removing from the sanctuary the sins which had been transferred to it by means of the ministration in the first apartment, Heb. 9:22,23; and that this work, in the antitype, commencing in 1844, occupies a brief but indefinite space, at the conclusion of which work of mercy for the world is finished.

**F.P.No. 13.** That as **the man of sin, the papacy,** has thought to change times and laws (the laws of God), Dan.7:25, and has misled almost all Christendom in regard to the fourth commandment; we find a prophecy of a reform in this respect to be wrought among believers just before the coming of Christ. Isa. 56:1,2; 1 Pet. 1:5; Rev. 14:12; etc.

**F.P.No. 18.** That the time of the cleansing of the sanctuary (see proposition 10), synchronizing with the time of the proclamation of the third angels message, is a time of the investigative judgment, first with reference to the dead, and at the close of probation with reference to the living; **to determine who of the myriads now sleeping in the dust of the**

**earth are worthy of a part in the first resur-
rection, and who of its living multitudes are
worthy of translation**--points which must be
determined before the Lord appears. (**Emphasis
supplied**).

A comparison with the Fundamental Beliefs
of Seventh-day Adventists as published in the
Church Manual 1986, reveals that the General
Conference has **"attacked"** the above principles
by making the following changes:-

1.  Deleted reference to Christ taking the
nature of Abraham's seed (Fundamental Belief,
No. 4).

2.  Confined the atonement to Christ's life,
suffering death and resurrection (Fundamental
Belief No. 9) and claims that Christ is now
"making available to believers the benefits
of His atoning sacrifice" (Fundamental Belief
No. 23).

3.  Deleted the term "most holy place" (Fundamental Belief No. 23).

4.  Presented the Investigative Judgment as
primarily a judgment of God to vindicate Him
before "heavenly intelligences" (Fundamental
Belief No. 23).

5.  Deleted all reference to the papacy as
"the man of sin" (as found in Fundamental Principle No. 13), thus snubbing the message of
the third angel of Revelation 14.

### EVOLUTION OF INVESTIGATIVE JUDGMENT

Let us briefly consider the underlying reasons
for the changes in Fundamental Belief No. 23,
as voted at the Dallas 1980 G.C. Session.
In the concluding portion of this statement

we read: "This judgment vindicates the justice of God in saving those who believe in Jesus"!

What a profound conclusion! Could we expect "heavenly intelligences" to have any other exp - ectation after watching God send His beloved Son into this world to be made sin, that He might save sinners? In Chapter 14, page 77 we noted the S.D.A. Bible Commentary quoting from the Spirit of Prophecy to show that "God's character had been vindicated before the universe" at the time of Christ's incarnation and death. Mrs White had also stated, "When Christ cried 'It is finished' the great sacrifice was complete. Satan and his angels were uprooted from the affection of the universe." (Signs of the Times, 23 Sept. 1889).

So why has the General Conference departed from its earlier belief? Why has the change come about only in recent times? Let us seek the answers by reverting to the year 1957.

This was a dramatic year for Adventism, which in retrospect, can be seen as a watershed in the doctrinal direction of our church. It started with the amazing revelation by Eternity magazine that the Seventh-day Adventist Church had been converted to Christianity. One of the reasons for this was our acceptance of a "completed atonement". In order to harmonise this position with the Spirit of Prophecy, an attempt was actually made to tamper with Mrs E.G. White's writings.

At this time, Elder M.L. Andreasen, the Chur- ch's proclaimed authority on our sanctuary mes- sage, had commenced writing letters to G.C. President Figuhr, protesting changes to our doctrines which he described as "new theology".

Early in 1957, the manuscript for the forth- coming book "Questions On Doctrine", was in the hands of the publishers. It would come off the press before the year-end and it would show to the world that we had changed sufficiently to be regarded as Christians. But would these changes be accepted by the S.D.A. church members and the ministry?

Thanks to the setting up of a "blue-print" college in Australia under the direction of the Spirit of Prophecy, the ministry in Australia was seen as orthodox. The workers were unlikely to be fooled by the heresies nestling among the truths in "Questions On Doctrine". So it was deemed advisable for Dr Le Roy Froom to visit Australia and forestall any fears that might be expressed by the ministry.

Fresh from recent dialogue with the Evangelicals, Froom would have been acutely aware of the precarious position in which the Church had arrived as a result of claiming to believe in a completed atonement.

Barnhouse had stated in no uncertain terms that to cling to our belief in Christ's further work for sinners in the Heavenly Sanctuary was "stale, flat and unprofitable" and that the doctrine of an investigative judgment to him was "the most colossal face saving phenomenon in religious history"! (Eternity, Sept. 1956).

This dilemma would be just one of the problems with which Froom could expect to be confronted. Apparently M.L. Andreasen saw such a problem as insoluble, for he was to write: "No Adventist can believe in a final atonement on the cross and remain an Adventist."

In the event, Froom made an extensive tour of Australia during the first half of the year 1957. Among the workers whom Froom counselled with at that time was a promising young man by the name of Desmond Ford. Just what thoughts

were exchanged between these men we do not know.
Shortly after Froom's visit to Australia an article appeared in the Australian "Signs of the Times" (24 June 1957) asking the question, "Do Believers and their sins come to judgment"? The question was answered in the affirmative; but on the back of this biblical truth was a free-loading interloper - "God has placed Himself on trial before the universe". The author of this article was Desmond Ford.

So now Adventists had been given two reasons for the investigative judgment. Probably this seedling of heresy went practically unnoticed, for surely it would have been immediately rooted out. Some eighteen years on (1975) President Pierson had been able to write of the investigative judgment, "The judgment separates those who merely begin to serve the Lord from those who follow Him unto the end" ("We Still Believe", p.124). No mention was made of God being placed on trial (See pp.148,149 of this book).

Meanwhile Ford was moulding the thinking of the ministry at Avondale College. Predictably, his interpretation of the first angel's message was soon being heard as young ministers began spreading the "good news" that God has to face up to a judgment. The seedling had grown and blossomed into the fruit of an heresy distinctly unique in the Christian world - that God could be judged and would be judged.

Such bold pronouncements as "God is up for judgment... God is in the hot seat" and "God is on trial more than men" have been cited on pages 76 and 132 of this book. Soon, some older ministers, who should have known better, began parroting these cliches - probably because they heard no dissenting voices from the leadership. Perhaps they saw Rev. 15:3,4 as supporting this

claim. If so, they failed to realize that a
judge comes to be seen as 'just and true' by the
way he has dispensed justice and mercy. In the
process, it is not he that has been on trial,
neither were the trials arranged for his benefit.
His reputation is consequential to the trials
which he has conducted.

So it is with God. "In the day of final judgment, every lost soul will understand the nature
of his own rejection of truth....Men will see
what their choice has been. Every question of
truth and error in the long-standing controversy
will then have been made plain. In the judgment
of the universe, God will stand clear of blame
for the existence or continuance of evil....When
the thoughts of all hearts shall be revealed,
both the loyal and rebellious will unite in
declaring, "Just and true are Thy ways, thou
King of saints. Who shall not fear Thee, O Lord,
and glorify Thy name?...for Thy judgments are
made manifest" Rev. 15:3,4; ("Desire of Ages"
p.58).

With the publication of "Seventh-day Adventists
Believe"...the evolution of Adventism's investigative judgment is taken one step further.
On page 326 we read a quotation from Holbrook's
"Light in the Shadows" p.34, "So a judgment
is needed - before the second coming of Christ
- to sift the true from the false and to demonstrate to the interested universe God's justice
in saving the sincere believer. **The issue is
with God and the universe, not between God and
the true child**" (Emphasis supplied).

Note the last sentence and compare this statement with Adventism's concept of the investigative judgment as expressed in Fundamental Principle No. 18. Or compare it with the following
quotations:-

"The ark that enshrines the tables of the law is covered with the mercy seat, before which Christ pleads His blood in the sinner's behalf" ("Great Controversy" p.415).

"Of one thing we may be sure, that as certainly as Christ once appeared to put away sin by the sacrifice of Himself, so surely is the judgment a definite feature of the great atoning work by which sin is put away" (C.H. Watson, "The Atoning Work of Christ", p.176).

"Christ had pledged to make men overcomers; He had 'guaranteed' this. It was no easy task; but the work of atonement was not finished until and unless He did it" (M.L.Andreasen, "Letters to the Churches" No. 6, 1959).

Would this sampling of Seventh-day Adventist thoughts on the investigative judgment, stressing the blood of atonement being applied on behalf of sinners, uphold the contention that the issue is not between God and the true child? No! Note that the blood atonement does not figure in an issue that "is with God and the universe".

As in Froom's book, "Movement Of Destiny", the blood atonement is left at the cross and we are told that, "now He makes available to all the benefits of this [His] atoning sacrifice" ("Seventh-day Adventist's Believe", p.313).

So in effect, the General Conference has destroyed the message of the first angel by altering the meaning of the judgment and putting God on trial. Therefore, the problem of a blood atonement in heaven in relation to a completed work of atonement at Calvary no longer remains as a point of contention with the Evangelicals. The message of the first angel becomes meaningless. It is destroyed. If there is no first angel, can there be a second and third angel? Hardly! This could explain the reason for the

Church's fascination with things Babylonian. How else could the General Conference consign Protestantism's traditional view of the beast of Revelation 13 to "the historical trash heap"!